Everything is peaceful.
You're relaxed in your favorite chair listening
to the newest record—and the phone rings!
"Hi, say I need your help."
It's the youth director at church. Since
you're feeling good you say, "Sure, what's up?"
"We need you for a counselor at camp.
It's just a week, you'll have about eight
or so kids. Will you do it?"
You say, yes, and hang up. Now all of a sudden
the magnitude of the job hits you.
"HELP! I'M A CAMP COUNSELOR," you yell.
Here's the book written to answer
whatever questions you may have.

HELP!
I'm a Camp Counselor

HELP! I'm a Camp Counselor

by H. Norman Wright

A Division of G/L Publications
Glendale, California, U.S.A.

Second Printing, 1969
Third Printing, 1971
Fourth Printing, 1973
Fifth Printing, 1976

Printed in U.S.A.

Published by
Regal Books Division, G/L Publications
Glendale, California 91209 U.S.A.

Library of Congress Catalog Card No. 68-18057

ISBN-0-8307-0032-3

CONTENTS

What's the Point?

Chapter 1

Never before in the history of our country has camping reached such a prominent place in the hearts and minds of individuals. Yet this is just the beginning, the "golden age" of camping has just begun. Camping has been on the uprise since the turn of the century. It has been used for personal and individual growth, and, in the Jugend camps that Hitler used to train young Germans, camping served a national purpose. There is a uniqueness to the Christian camping program that sets it apart from others: It seeks to develop the total person, not only in relationship to himself and others, but also to God. Thus his life has a purpose. There is the possibility of a complete change taking place in the individual.

Campers, both young and old, can become aware of the presence of God as they establish a new sensitivity toward the creation of God. They are able to see and appreciate the beauty of nature which God has made and established. The change of pace in their daily life and environment makes them more perceptive and observant. The well-established plan and order of God in his creation is evident as they see the marvels of nature. Through this awareness and the program of the camp, individuals are led to see God's perfect plan in the person of Jesus Christ.

Because Christ is central in the camping program, campers of all ages may come to meet him face to face for the first time, and others may renew in a living, vital way their relationship with God. Christian campers come to camp looking for solutions to their problems. They come looking for challenge and enrichment that will enable them to be leaders in the Christian faith and community. They come looking for guidance so that they are able to maintain an unbroken fellowship with Jesus Christ when they return home. They want to know how to live and survive as Christians! They face and learn to handle these questions and others, by learning in actual life situations at camp rather than in the formal teaching situation. Christ is presented through informal teaching. Camp, in one sense, is a training ground for Christian principles. A place where relationships are learned, tested and tried.

Learning takes place each moment the camper is awake and the educators are not just the speakers but each staff member, the environment, and the other campers.

Camping will offer an opportunity for achieving the Christian education objectives of the local church program. The evidence over the years has indicated that camp is one of the most powerful and effective tools in the development of the total Christian person.

The goals of Christian camping vary from camp to camp and from church to church. The Philosophy Committee of the National Sunday School Association Camp Commissions has provided a suggested list.

"The Christian camp should provide opportunities:

(1) to deal with campers as individuals, counseling them personally in the areas of their spiritual need (note Jesus' example in John 3-5);

(2) to encourage definite spiritual decision at the level of the camper's readiness (as in Jesus' example in the same chapters in John);

(3) to help establish good habits of Christian living —prayer, Bible reading and study, personal devotions and witnessing (II Timothy 3:14-17; Acts 1:8; 2:42);

(4) to have practical experience in leadership, service, witnessing and application of spiritual truths to daily living (II Timothy 2:2; John 13:1-17; Luke 22:24-28; Mark 6:7).

"In addition, the Christian camp seeks other outcomes related to the total development of the camper, such as:

(1) the establishment of sound health habits—cleanliness, adequate rest, proper diet, wholesome exercise and good attitudes toward the body as God's temple (I Corinthians 6:19,20);

(2) the profitable and wise use of leisure, independent of artificial machine-made amusements (Ephesians 5:15,16);

(3) learning outdoor skills as a means of developing character and as training for possible future missionary work (I Corinthians 9:19-27; 10-31);

(4) development of the ability to get along with others unselfishly (I Corinthians 13; Romans 12:9-21);

(5) learning effective leadership skills (Exodus 35:30-35);

(6) learning responsibility for one's own decisions (Galatians 6:4-9)."*

*Reprinted from "Guiding Principles for Christian Camping," National Sunday School Association, Wheaton, Illinois."

Who . . . Me?

Chapter 2

Each year, thousands of children and youth attend camp and the experiences of this time have a lasting effect and influence upon their development and total life perspective. The location of the camp, the atmosphere of the physical surroundings, the quality of the food, the thrust and message of the speakers—all these contribute to the camp experience, and yet the factor or element that very often exerts the most influence upon the camper is you, the counselor.

Counseling at camp will present many opportunities to you as well as presenting certain requirements. Why should you consider camp counseling? What are the benefits, the challenge, the requirements and the cost? What will you have to do and what will you have to learn? Questions like these flicker through your mind when you are confronted with the invitation and challenge of a counseling experience. What will the camp experience mean and do for you? One of the values of being at camp for a weekend or summer is the enjoyment of the beautiful surroundings that God has created. There will be memories of the clear sky during the day and the vast expanse of sparkling stars in the evening. Thoughts of swimming in the pool or lake, canoeing, hiking up the trail or exploring new regions, amusing experiences with other counselors and campers, the challenge and learning of the meetings, that last bite of food at the snack shop in the evening, the fun and skit time where you ended up with the pie in the face; this is a part of camping.

As a person and a leader, you will grow, learn, make mistakes and profit from them. Far more important, you will have the satisfaction of knowing that you have been used as an instrument of God to help mold and develop the life of a child or young person. The experience of leading a person to a saving knowledge of Jesus Christ can never be surpassed by any other experience. To lead the camper to discover the Christian life, to assist him to grow, to help him find God's will for his life—these are experiences that you will never forget.

What is a camp counselor? You are one who is in the position of giving an opinion, recommendation or advice for purpose or direction. You help and guide by word and deed. You have had a genuine experience with Jesus Christ and know the redeeming work of God in your life. You have a God-given love for children and young people and a genuine concern for their many problems. Two assets which are almost mandatory are the ability to camp and to counsel. The ability to counsel means to be interested in people. Because your main concern in camp is with people, you assume several roles.

A TEACHER You are a teacher in the sense that your attitudes and actions are observed and either copied or reacted to by your campers. You are a teacher in that you are involved in direct instruction. Campers realize that counselors are people and have faults. Therefore, they don't expect perfection. They will learn from you anyway, but they'll learn more if you admit that you know you're not perfect and show them that you try to improve. Your actions and attitudes toward others will teach with an impact. Your classroom is your dorm, the dinner table, the athletic field, the meeting hall and the chapel. Use it well!

A FRIEND As a friend, you are interested in each camper, his likes and dislikes, his problems, his experiences and you accept him or learn to accept him for what he is. You are friendly, a good listener and approachable, but at the same time, you avoid the danger of being too familiar. The camper learns to trust and to share his most intimate thoughts and fears and this he does, when he knows that his confidence won't be broken. This relationship of a friend, however, exists on an adult-to-camper level.

Campers don't respect the counselor who attempts to act on the camper's age level. There arises the danger of being so much "in" with the kids that they think of you as one of them and not as a leader. Campers do not want you to act as they do. You are an adult and as such should command their regard and respect. Establish yourself in their minds as a leader if you are going to lead them. If you become one of the campers, your effectiveness will be greatly reduced.

ADMINISTRATOR AND ORGANIZER You will be involved in the actual running of the camp and can expect to be called upon to help with administrative duties if the need arises. This could involve anything from organizing and running an athletic program to assisting in the business office. It can also involve camper records and camp evaluation forms.

The organization phase may appear in your relations with your campers. Many decisions are needed in the course of a camp and campers need someone to give them the direction necessary in order to make many of these decisions. Some campers will be able to develop their own organization for teams, cabin cleanup, problems that arise, but others will find it necessary to rely upon your advice and counsel. Organization that comes from the counselor comes in the form of suggestions and recommendations, questions and honest concern. In cases of planning for certain activities and functions, the campers can be encouraged to assume the responsibility for much of this. You can plan for the camp but you do not plan the camp.

A SPIRITUAL LEADER Have you ever considered yourself in this role before? Needless to say, it may very well be a new role for you. You will minister to the needs of others for a change instead of having others minister to you. This ministry of spiritual leadership is vital—it is the reason you are a counselor. In a sense, you'll be offering to the camper the spiritual strength that you have. You will have to be under the control and direction of God. Your ministry will involve praying with and for each of your campers. You will worship with them and search the Scriptures with them and attempt to answer their questions or guide them to someone who can. You will be "sharing God" with the campers. Through you, they will see the Christian life in action.

So counseling involves many jobs or roles, and camps and conferences will be only as effective as its counselors. Before you take the position, it is well to realize that the success of the conference in terms of human instrumentality will always rest with the counselor more than with any other one person. It is through your personal interest, concern and friendliness that you will earn, in a very special way, the right, as well as the opportunity, to talk with a child or young person about his relationship with Jesus Christ. Speakers will be influential and will be used of God to provoke thought. Through their messages, the Holy Spirit will work to bring conviction and sense of need. But in most cases, you will be the one, who discusses, questions, prays, presents and points out Scripture to the inquirer and who is involved in the direct follow-up program. This is a momentous responsibility but also a wonderful privilege.

Your value in the camping program cannot be overestimated. A speaker may fail to communicate, the program may be disorganized, but with good counselors, it will make little difference. You can make or break the camp and the camper.

A camp is not a vacation and anyone who uses a counseling experience for this purpose shouldn't attend. It's a job and a ministry. Your time is never your own; it belongs to your campers. There will be constant demands upon you as counseling is VERY strenuous and demands all of your resources.

WHAT SHOULD YOU BE? Well qualified counselors are essential to a successful camp program. As you consider this wonderful area of ministry, camp counseling, ask yourself what will your campers see? What are you like? What should you be like?

The best qualifications are those of Christ himself: his love and patience, his poise, his peace, his strength and gentleness, his insight and understanding of human nature are what you desire. As you grow in your day-by-day walk and relationship with Jesus Christ, these will be manifest more and more.

The individual who teaches by example and is consistent enough to practice what he believes is a candidate for becoming a successful worker with pliable and impressionable campers. Your personal life, including philosophy, attitudes and beliefs, are constantly on trial and examination by the campers, camp staff, speakers, director and fellow counselors. Everything you are, say and do will be observed. Should your talk about your dates or behavior be heard by the campers? How do you react when your cabin loses a ball game? Respect is never demanded and gained but won and earned by the depth of your own personal life.

What is the quality of your spiritual life? If you wait until camp to begin a regular systematic devotional life you will be unable to minister to your campers. Your relationship with Jesus Christ must be a constant, real, meaningful experience that is well established. Sincerity of convictions and adherence to the New Testament teachings, interpersonal relationships are qualities that you should strive after. The real test of your spiritual life quite often comes into focus when problems arise in camp. This is where Christianity is real, and it can stand the test!

Knowledge of the Scriptures, the ability to pray before others, being able to answer basic questions about your faith and the ability to lead another person to Christ—these are just a few of the tests that will be yours when you counsel.

Camp directors and staffs are constantly on the lookout for people with that quality called "being positive." A positive attitude is contagious, especially in camp. In a sense, you are really a salesman. You sell campers on everything—food, speakers, accommodations, program, athletics, crafts and your purpose for the camp. Even the presenting of Jesus Christ in a positive manner is important. And there is no other way in which to present him!

Enthusiasm is one way of being positive. Being enthusiastic about the meetings, the meals, in fun around the tables, in the recreational events and athletic competition, cabin-inspection rivalry. When you ask questions positively, you'll get your campers in the habit of saying "yes" and you'll be surprised how this attitude catches on with the others.

A counselor without the quality of love is not a counselor. Your love must have its basis in the love that God presented to you in Jesus Christ. Your love for others begins with your love for him.

Your love must be displayed in very practical ways toward your campers. They'll know if it is real and genuine or manufactured. Kind words are readily accepted but without kind deeds, they are empty. Real patience, sympathy, empathy, understanding go hand in hand with love. Some children and adolescents aren't as easy to love as others. You may be repulsed because of physical deformities or personality disorders.

Some campers will forever be getting into trouble and disrupting meetings and sleep! Others are overly verbal and are constantly talking. There are those who never let you out of their sight. Some of them will attempt to "needle you" or "bug you" constantly simply because you represent authority or because they don't like you. Can you love these campers? You'll have to, for they are in camp because of a need in their lives. You have the responsibility and challenge of trying to meet this need. In many cases, they're more in need of love than the average individual in your group. This demands all the patience that you can muster, but more than that, it requires a complete dependence upon Jesus Christ for strength, insight and love that only he can give you to impart to each hungry individual.

Someone once said that the humble person is a much-sought-after creature but is seldom found. His species is becoming extinct. Too many Christians today talk about having humility before God but fail to have any before man. As you counsel and talk with your group, talk about their lives, their friends, their education, hobbies and problems. Most people dislike to hear the person who cannot talk about anyone but himself. Campers tire of the counselor who attempts to impress or shock them by a constant barrage of personal experiences. Time is short and precious when you're at camp—use it well.

If you give any personal examples or experiences, don't be guilty of dragging out your "past life" before meeting Christ, as though you were proud of it. An example of this was evident one evening as a youth speaker told of his activities as a "hood and gangster" before becoming a Christian. Over two-thirds of the message was spent in giving precise details of his notorious past and associations and how he had never been caught and convicted. The last few moments of the message recalled his conversion experience and the change that had taken place in his life through the encounter that he had with Jesus Christ. When the meeting ended several of the youth were heard to comment, "Man, he really lived it up, didn't he"; "hey, he sure had the gay time before he was a Christian." Then one person asked the question, "I wonder why he gets off without paying for any of those crimes? Is that the way it should be? It just doesn't seem right to me." The fact that this man met Christ and was a changed person didn't register with the audience because he had dwelt so much on his past. The attention-getters that we sometimes use can have a negative effect.

Personal habits are very necessary in the close living atmosphere of a camp. Tidiness with appearance, clothes, personal belongings do much to instill these same habits with your group. Do you clean up the area around your bunk and put things away? Getting to camp isn't an invitation to wear out all the old sloppy clothes that you have, nor is it an excuse to endeavor to smell like the mules or horses that you ride. Campers will imitate you. They will pick up any bad habits that you might exhibit. Are your table manners worth copying? If you're boisterous and use slang, complaining or boastful, unkempt and slovenly, expect the same to develop as you set the pattern!

A basic attribute of common intelligence is helpful to the counseling situation. It is almost essential to understand, guide and make adjustments to campers and the total camp program. If you have difficulty making decisions or knowing what is good common sense, or what isn't, then camp counseling can be a nightmare for you. Camps aren't looking for superior ratings when it comes to the intelligence factor, but they do want those who can make decisions and are sensible in their approach to everyday situations and problems.

A stable character and pleasant personality are

necessities if you are to command respect and be an example that others will emulate. One who attempts to understand opposing points of view is a definite asset to the camping program. Some counselors have been more of a problem than the campers because of moodiness. You can't remain aloof in camp without affecting everyone and the total atmosphere of the camp. A real liking and interest in people and the enjoyment of being around them is something that each fledgling counselor must consider. If a negative reaction to this idea is present, camp counseling will be difficult. Camp life consists of living with people for twenty-four hours a day and each person is different.

Some camp experiences have actually been destroyed by a single counselor. This has come about when the counselor wasn't aware of some shortcomings in his own life and created more problems than was thought possible. Too many counselors come to camp conscious of some problems, personality deviation, or uncontrollable habits, but unwilling to do anything to correct them. If you fit into this category and are thinking of taking a position at a camp, whether it is for a summer or a weekend, disqualify yourself as a counselor and seek help. The one thing that you try to hide from others may be the same problem area one of your campers has. If he seeks you out and asks your help and advice, what will you be able to say or do? Honesty is a characteristic that is mandatory here. If a problem exists, be willing to admit it to yourself and to someone else who can aid and assist you.

Emotional maturity and stability are your close friends. To maintain control at all times, to carry on an even relationship with other staff members, to be self confident and to accept and profit from criticism, are all factors that are a part of emotional maturity.

If you are planning to counsel for an entire summer, this means leaving the family and friends, your "steady," your favorite haunts and activities and your church. Can you be unaffected by absence from all of these? Do you have a nervous system that is able to stand the noise and stress of living with young, exuberant campers? Consider these before you undertake an extended counseling experience. If you decide to leave the camp during the middle of the season, you will affect the camp program and entire staff.

Reliability and adaptability are two key concepts that camp directors are very keen about. The work of running a camp is so much easier if the director can depend upon his staff, even when he isn't present. Counselors who are willing to abide by the rules that the camp has established are at a premium. The task of operating a camp involves work on the part of all staff members. Counselors who have a genuine interest in their work will cheerfully do more than what has been assigned to them. This involves working by yourself and with others. Mature counselors have the ability to sense and assume responsibility without having to be told everything.

Most camps have standards of behavior established not only for counselors but for the campers as well. The responsibility for seeing that all campers (not just your own) follow these standards falls upon you. This was pointed out in a camp situation where the effectiveness of the camp was almost totally ruined because of some counselors failing to take responsibility. Several of the couples at this high school camp had become too "chummy" and during the free time sat around in plain sight of everyone. Several counselors passed by but said, "Well, that's not my problem. They're not my campers. Their counselor ought to be around to see that!" And when confronted with this later, the reply was "Well, no one told me to handle that situation. It wasn't my responsibility. They have their own counselors." This is not the type of attitude that should prevail. Seek to maintain the standards of the camp with any and all campers. . . . this is the responsibility a counselor should assume.

Because a camp experience involves many people, situations arise which necessitate change. Camps seek out individuals who have the ability to adjust to new and varied situations and those who can accept responsibility for many tasks. The person who can work well with others who perhaps have "rough edges" on their personalities will contribute greatly to establishing a harmonious atmosphere among staff members.

A sickly counselor is a hazard to those around him. Personal health standards are usually maintained by each camp and counselors above all must have good health and seek to maintain this while at camp. If you become ill or have an accident, seek out the camp nurse or physician immediately. This not only helps to ensure your health but is a strong motivating factor for campers to do the same. Health and safety consciousness is a standard that is continuous in its application.

Lack of sleep is one detriment to good health that you will face. Know your sleep requirement and attempt to meet it. Any attempt to compensate for lack of sleep must be done at a time when it doesn't hurt the camp program nor take you away from your duties.

Sincere interest in camping and the camp where you are serving will enable you to maintain a proper attitude and perspective about your work. Some people love camping when the weather is bright and clear and insects are a rarity, but do you still have the same feelings about camp when it rains for two days and the mosquitoes make your sleep miserable? This is all a part of counseling. How you react to these problems will direct the reaction of your campers. Each camp and conference grounds is unique and has its established traditions, goals and policies. You will do well to know and understand the traditions, ideals and objectives of the camp, the policies as they pertain to staff and camper relationships and operational standards, the procedures for beginning and closing camp, and the area immediately surrounding the camp.

These are just some of the qualities and characteristics that are sought after by the camp director. How do you measure up to these? Many years ago a study was undertaken which indicated that certain characteristics tended to be identified with the better counselors. These qualities haven't changed throughout the years:

Executive ability and dispatch.
Ability to foresee consequences of conduct.
Ability and thoroughness in analyzing problems and situations.
Ability to formulate clearly specific objectives for campers.
Ability to get campers to propose, plan, initiate, execute and evaluate enterprises.
Ability to help campers face issues that arise in living together in the camp community.
Ability to use cooperative rather than autocratie methods of control.
Ability to extend and enlarge campers' interests.
Ability to deal intelligently with difficult campers.
Constructive participation in leaders' meetings.*

Campers, too, have had the opportunity to express themselves concerning the type of counselors that they favor. It is well to consider yourself from this perspective. At camp, you'll need to try to project yourself into the camper's situation and consider it from his viewpoint. See how he views you and what you say. Campers have stated that they like counselors who can be approached. In other words, they can talk with them and can get close to them. A friendly counselor is one who will be liked. Being agreeable (within limits) is another favorable trait along with being sympathetic and

*Physical Ed, and Recreation, Benson-Goldberg, (page 44). Hendry, C. E., "A Cooperative Study of Counselors" Association Boys' Work Journal, May, 1931.

understanding. Campers want counselors who are strict and can maintain order. There are times when you'd never believe this to hear them talk and complain, but inwardly they desire this type of leader. Coupled with this, however, is the liking of a person who isn't unnecessarily severe, who isn't domineering and "bossy" and one who is fair and has no favorites in camp. They are also favorably inclined toward the person who participates in all of their activities with them.

How will you fit in as a counselor? Sounds a bit terrifying doesn't it? And yet what a tremendous challenge. A weekend counseling at your own church camp or a week or even a summer at a conference grounds will permanently affect your life and will deepen your commitment to Jesus Christ.

A method of rating yourself as a prospective counselor has been presented in "Camp Counseling" by Viola Mitchell and Ida Crawford.*

This form can be a valuable tool, not only for you, but for the camp and entire counseling staff. There are three methods of usage. After you have completed the form, you may use this as a guide to better understand yourself and strive for improvement in the weaker areas. Some camps keep the forms on file for the counselor and during the camping season, the camp director discusses the results with the counselor.

Another method is perhaps the most beneficial. Small groups of counselors meet together so you can share with one another how you rated yourself on the individual questions. Then the others in the group tell the one who has just shared how they would rate him on the same form. Honest appraisal by others can be very helpful and revealing, but it takes a complete openness and a willingness to be objective about yourself.

HOW DO YOU RATE?

If you would like to know your possibilities for success and enjoyment as a counselor, rate yourself on the tests which follow. Remember that there is nothing to be gained by "cheating" on them for the real proof comes when you begin working with fellow staff members and campers on the job.

Check each trait in the proper column; then connect them with a solid line to indicate your "profile." Note where your weaknesses lie as the line slumps off to the left and also assess your strengths as the line bears triumphantly to the right.

HEALTH	Poor 1	Below Average 2	Average 3	Above Average 4	Superior 5
1. Stamina enough to last through a strenuous day					
2. Well-balanced meals eaten regularly					
3. Regular sleep in sufficient quantity					

	Poor	Below Average	Average	Above Average	Superior
	1	2	3	4	5
4. No smoking					
5. No intoxicating liquors					
6. Sufficient vigorous exercise each day					
7. Pleasing and neat appearance					
8. Cleanliness of person and clothing					
9. Graciousness and mannerliness					
10. Tact (speak truthfully, but without unnecessarily offending or hurting others)					
11. Cooperativeness (even when carrying out the plans of others)					
12. Cheerfulness (no sulking or moodiness)					
13. Sense of humor (even when the joke's on you)					
14. Good English (no profanity or excess slang)					
15. Warmth (a friendly personality that attracts others to you)					
16. Poise (even in emergencies or embarrassing situations)					

	Poor	Below Average	Average	Above Average	Superior
	1	2	3	4	5
17. Appreciation of the beautiful in deed, music, nature and literature					
18. Sincere liking for campers (even unattractive and "naughty" ones)					
19. Enjoyment of hard work (even when it means getting your clothing dirty)					
20. Skills and knowledge of outdoor living (in rain, as well as sunshine)					
21. Adaptability (can happily change plans to fit in with others or the weather)					
22. Can "take" as well as "give" orders					
23. Love of fun (can see possibilities for enjoyment in almost any situation)					
24. Interested in many things					
25. Specialization (ability to "do" at least one camp activity well)					
26. Initiative (ability to start without outside prodding or suggestion)					

	Poor	Below Average	Average	Above Average	Superior
	1	2	3	4	5
27. Promptness at all appointments and in performing all tasks					
28. Dependability (do what you say you will when you say you will)					
29. Industry (constantly up and doing)					
30. Persistence (finish what you start with dispatch and thoroughness)					
31. Curiosity (want to know about many things just for the sake of knowing)					
32. Neatness (keep own living quarters neat and clean)					

EMOTIONAL MATURITY

"When I was a child, I spake as a child, . . . but when I became a man, I put away childish things" is not necessarily true of all adults. A person who harbors childish traits is said to be emotionally immature, and, though frequently at a loss to understand why, he is often unhappy, for his behavior keeps him at constant odds with himself and his associates. He often feels mistreated and deprived of his just dues. Camp directors look upon a counselor's degree of emotional maturity as one of the surest indices of his probable success. You can scarcely expect to fulfill your job of helping your campers mature unless you can set an example.

Your physical and mental maturity tell nothing of your emotional maturity. The fact that you are strong as an ox or fleet as a deer does not indicate that you have learned to face up to life squarely and solve your problems in an adult way. Indeed, you may be a straight "A" student at school and still be unable to apply any of your intelligence to solve your own problems and help you deal more effectively with people.

How often we hear some exasperated person say to another "Why don't you grow up?" What actions and attitudes determine maturity? Why is one person labeled mature and another immature? First of all, a mature person has awakened to the fact that every person around him has wants and needs similar to his own and he therefore cannot always have his own way. For instance, if you have set your heart on doing something with a particular buddy on your day off, you don't sulk, try to get even, or throw a tantrum if you find your pal has made other plans or that unforseen developments have made it necessary for one of you to remain on duty in camp. You try to persuade others to your way of thinking but you do it by reasoning with them, not by pouting, wheedling, flattering or making yourself so disagreeable that others give in rather than suffer the consequences.

When someone with obviously good intentions criticizes something about you, you are smart enough to analyze the remark and profit by any truth there is in it, instead of flaring up pigheadedly at the thought that another should even hint that you are anything less than perfect. You have pride and faith in yourself yet display a becoming modesty and don't feel it necessary to alibi for every shortcoming. You aren't a doormat who lets everyone walk over you at will; you may even on occasion rise up in righteous anger or resentment about things important enough to really matter.

You enjoy the feeling of being able to influence others but don't misuse this ability. You exercise it only to lead in right directions but avoid carrying it to the point where you make willing slaves of others and have them groveling at your feet. You don't try to run peoples' lives but, instead, try to do a good job of running your own. You organize your daily living with a good balance of work, play, laughter, seriousness and all other components of the good life. You can fit easily into the routine of camp living, accepting reasonable camp rules cheerfully because you know they are meant to protect the best interests of all. Most of all, you are thoughtful of others and considerate of their needs and wishes.

The real criterion is that the emotionally immature person governs his actions by his emotions whereas the mature person keeps his reasoning power instead of his emotions in the driver's seat at all times.

EMOTIONAL MATURITY

	Poor 1	Below Average 2	Average 3	Above Average 4	Superior 5
1. Can you accept criticism without undue anger or hurt, acting upon it if justified, disregarding it if not?					
2. Are you tolerant of others and willing to overlook their faults?					
3. Do you feel genuinely happy at the success of others and sincerely congratulate them?					
4. Do you refrain from listening to and repeating undue gossip about others?					
5. Do you converse about other things and persons? Test it by checking your conversation to see how frequently you use the pronoun "I"					
6. Are you altruistic, often putting the welfare and happiness of others above your own?					
7. Do you refrain from emotional outbursts of anger, tears, etc.?					
8. Do you face disagreeable duties promptly and without trying to escape by playing sick or making excuses?					
9. Can you stay away from home a month or more without undue homesickness?					

	Poor	Below Average	Average	Above Average	Superior
	1	2	3	4	5
10. Can you weigh facts and make decisions promptly, then abide by your decisions?					
11. Are you willing to postpone things you want to do now in favor of greater benefits or pleasure later?					
12. Are you usually on good terms with your family and associates?					
13. When things go wrong, can you objectively determine the cause and remedy it without alibiing for yourself and blaming it on other people or things?					
14. When disagreeing with another, can you discuss it calmly and usually work out a mutually satisfactory agreement without hard feelings?					
15. Can you enter into informal social events of many types wholeheartedly?					
16. Do you really enjoy doing little things for others, even though you know they will likely go unknown and unappreciated?					

	1 Poor	2 Below Average	3 Average	4 Above Average	5 Superior
17. Do you dress neatly and modestly without tendency to gaudiness or overdress?					
18. Can you dismiss past sins and mistakes that can't be remedied now without dwelling on them?					
19. Can you make decisions regarding others objectively, disregarding your personal dislike or resentment of them?					
20. As a leader, do you work democratically without dictating or forcing your will on others?					
21. Are you loyal to your friends, minimizing or not mentioning their faults to others?					
22. Are you free from "touchiness," so that others do not have to handle you with kid gloves?					
23. Do you act according to your honest convictions regardless of what others may think or say about it?					
24. Do you have a kindly feeling toward most people, a deep affection for some, and no unhealthy attachments to any?					

	Poor	Below Average	Average	Above Average	Superior
	1	2	3	4	5
25. Do you feel that you usually get about what you deserve? Are you free from a feeling that others "have it in for" you?					

In order to make a rough estimate of your overall emotional maturity, total all scores and divide by 25 (the number of items rated). If you have proceeded honestly and objectively, an average of 4 or 5 means you are quite acceptable, 3 indicates you are average, and a 1 or 2 shows that you are below average and should "grow up." Here are some suggestions to help you attain emotional maturity:

1. Face your deficiencies frankly and resolve to eradicate them just as quickly and completely as possible.

2. Set out to acquire definite skills and interests which have social rather than selfish or personal values.

3. Make it a point to associate with a number of emotionally mature people. Observe them and try to determine why they are so.*

*Mitchell and Crawford: *Camp Counseling*, 3rd edition. Philadelphia, W. B. Saunders Co., 1961. Pages 40-44.

4. If you feel a need for help, seek someone qualified and discuss the problem frankly and openly with him. Be willing to act on his recommendations even though they're not flattering.

5. Get wrapped up in causes so big and worthwhile that they completely absorb you, making you forget yourself and your troubles.

Before you begin your counseling at a camp, whether it be a weekend, week or entire summer, you should know something about the camp and what is expected of you. These are questions to ask yourself about your position:

1. Is a job description available so you may know what is expected of you?
2. Do you know what this camp is like in its physical facilities, layout and camp boundaries?
3. Do you know how the camp is organized, the line and staff relationships?
4. Have the camp objectives been clarified to you and are you in agreement with them?
5. What are your responsibilities to the campers, other staff members, director and church (if counseling for a particular church)?
6. What free time do you have at camp and what provisions are made for personal use of equipment?
7. Are you insured? What are the arrangements for friends or family who may come to visit? If you are to be paid, what is the amount and when?
8. Who is your immediate superior?
9. What age group will you be counseling and will any information be made available concerning the campers' background?

10. Are there any records or reports that you'll be required to keep?

11. Are Bible study and follow-up material available to you from the camp itself or are you to bring your own?

12. What are the standards that the camp expects you to maintain?

13. What type of follow-up program does this camp use and will you be able to carry this out?

14. Will the camp train you in areas in which you are weak and inexperienced?

Togetherness?

Chapter 3

Several years ago the afternoon train pulled into a small Quaker town in Pennsylvania, and a stranger alighted. He walked over to one of the people on the platform and said, "What type of town is this, and what kind of people live here?"

"What kind of place did you come from, and what were the people like who lived there?" the Quaker replied.

"They were hard people to get along with, and the town was noisy."

"This is the same kind of town, and the same kind of people." The stranger got back on the train.

The next afternoon when the train pulled in, off hopped another stranger. Smiling, he approached the group on the platform and cheerily said, "Hi, there! I'm looking for a town to live in permanently. What do you have here?"

Once more the Quaker replied, "Where did you come from, and what were the people like?"

"I came from a happy place, and the people were kind and friendly."

"You'll find the same conditions here," said the Quaker.

"Good! I need a place like this to live. Will you help me get settled?"

"Sure!" chorused the group.

Your attitudes are an indication of what you may expect in others. Knowing when and how to give is the secret of getting along with other people.

Getting along with others and working harmoniously with them is going to be your responsibility while at camp. Interpersonal relationships among counselors and other staff members influence camp morale.

MEET THE BOSS

If you think that you do an unlimited amount of work at camp, take over the job of camp director for a season and you'll find out what work really is! The camp director usually spends many weeks and months in advance preparation. He is responsible for the entire camp and is concerned with each person whether he be dishwasher, counselor, camper, speaker or maintenance worker. His job is complex and momentous, and he has more problems and responsibilities than you have ever thought possible. The last problem he wants is a difficult counselor. In a sense, your job is to make his easier by carrying out your duties to the fullest, and by not creating any additional work. Loyalty to the camp director is expected of all staff workers.

If there is a difference of opinion concerning the camp policies or program, and the manner in which things are done, go straight to the camp director and talk to him about the problem. He will appreciate a direct approach rather than hearing about it through the "grapevine." It is easy to be critical of rules and regulations but sometimes difficult to carry them out in a spirit of cheerfulness and understanding.

Don't ask for special favors. Standards and consistent decisions are an important factor in maintaining good morale.

You have been asked to be a counselor because you have the ability to make decisions and to deal with problems. There will be occasions when you'll wonder whether to tackle a problem or ask for help and assistance. Any minor difficulties should be handled by you but those that take special training and advice might be out of your jurisdiction. Quite often, a camp will have a men's dean and women's dean or assistant camp director in charge of counselors. These are the people to seek out first instead of going directly to the camp director. If they are unable to assist, they will say so and then have you contact the director.

Camp directors expect you, the counselor, to be

efficient, prompt, enthusiastic, cooperative, capable of handling work, prompt in turning in all reports, good conduct out of camp in all situations that will reflect on camp, and well-trained for the specific job that you have.

MEET YOUR COLLEAGUES

The quality of the camp staff will determine the camp morale. If tensions and animosities exist between counselors, campers will be swift to perceive this and in some cases, capitalize upon the fact. You will actually have to work at fitting into the group, and in some instances go out of your way to establish new friendships.

Don't wait for the other counselor to make the first approach, but be outgoing with all fellow workers. Friendliness can be contagious. Most of us, however, wait to catch it from someone else, instead of giving the other person the opportunity to catch it from us. Don't wait around to see if people will like you, but just assume that they will. Don't wait for them to be the first to say "hello" or to smile. Take the lead and be friendly and they will follow. If everyone waits around for someone to make the first overture, the atmosphere can become very uncomfortable and cool. People relax when someone puts himself out by breaking the ice. Cliques and special favorites among counselors can have a dire effect upon everyone. Total involvement will be more advantageous to you and the entire group.

Gossip and chance comments have a way of

filtering back to the person involved. By the time they arrive, they're usually distorted and even worse than when first said. How would you react if you picked up the information that another counselor had slandered you? Probably, you would feel like retaliating and this would then add fuel to the fire, and perhaps explode in a disruptive way that would affect the outcome of the camp! If you have a grievance against someone and are unable to understand him, try to see things from his viewpoint. Pray about the problem and the person. Then talk with him directly! If the situation still exists, ask for assistance from your superior.

If you have a complaint concerning the quality of work done by others, be sure that yours is above reproach! Forget the remarks that you hear about other staff members. Encourage the speaker to solve the problem by other means. Remember, though, that you can't solve all problems by yourself. A regular, meaningful prayer life helps overcome seemingly insurmountable difficulties.

Privacy is a rarity at camp and the private moments that you have are cherished. Be sure to consider the privacy of others, not only the individual but also his property and belongings. It is the best policy not to borrow or lend personal articles, clothing or money. Towns and supply stores are close at hand.

A counseling staff that cooperates with one another, is unselfish in interest and work, exhibits patience, tact, friendliness, loyalty and openmindedness, will see the results in the quality of the camp and the lives of the campers. Set aside some time during the week when you and the other counselors can get together for Bible study, prayer and a sharing of problems.

Perhaps you've had some experience counseling. If so, you can be a tremendous asset to the novice. You know the administrative policies and routines of camp. You may have special techniques that have aided you in handling campers. Sharing of your experiences in a helpful and humble way can save hours of frustration for the new counselor.

Don't hesitate to give credit, appreciation and encouragement. If someone is deserving of a compliment, give it to him. In fact, go out of your way to do so. Too many people are tight-lipped with their words of praise. It isn't difficult to find an achievement that merits praise. If you look for the little things, instead of the big ostentatious feats, you'll find much more to commend a person. Many people are uncertain about themselves, and you may give them the reassurance they need. Encouragement, patience, willingness to listen, praise when deserved, and small constructive doses of criticism, will help this new fellow worker.

There is no place in the camping program for sarcasm or harassment. New counselors may be inexpert or ineffective at times, but they can learn if given the opportunity and encouragement. Include all your colleagues in discussions and decisions.

If you are a new counselor don't hesitate to consult the experienced person, but avoid the danger of becoming overly dependent.

Realize also that visits by friends from home are subject to the policy of the camp. They can be seen on your time off. Usually they have to seek accommodations away from camp.

Another area of concern is that of boy-girl relationships. Each camp will have its own policy concerning dating activities between women and men counselors. Any relationships here set an example for the entire camp. You will be carefully observed and discussed by the campers! Frequent upsets between counselors who are going together can hamper testimony and effectiveness. Be careful of match-making between counselors. Campers quickly pick this up and soon the information, whether true or not, is spread throughout the entire camp. At no time should you date campers.

MEET YOUR RESPONSIBILITIES

One way to initiate good interpersonal relationships with your campers is to start out on the right foot. Greet the campers in a friendly manner and let them know that you are happy that they'll be in your cabin. Show that you are interested in them and what they like, perhaps by asking questions. Be sure to learn their names as soon as possible.

Perhaps it is a real climb up the hill to the cabins. Don't be one of those who stands and laughs at the pathetic struggle of some camper as he attempts to tote, drag, push or even roll his belongings toward his home for the week. Ask if you can help, but don't jump in and grab the gear. He may prefer doing it his way, regardless of how it looks to you.

Let the campers know the schedule, camp procedure, necessary rules concerning all phases of camp life and let them ask questions concerning these. Use some of the old campers to help orient the novices, but work closely with them so they learn how to do this properly. Let the campers discuss with you what they are seeking at camp and what they like to do. This will certainly aid you as you work with them.

Participate in all camp activities with them from kitchen K.P., to devotions, to cleaning the dorm, to playing a game of softball. In lieu of ordering the campers to follow established rules, work and play with them to show them the routine and framework of camp. To join the campers on an assignment, or work project is much more effective than telling them.

The facilities are there for the enjoyment and use of campers and counselors, but most camps indicate that campers should have the first opportunity to use them. This concerns swimming pool, tennis, volleyball and basketball courts, baseball diamonds, ping pong tables and arts and crafts materials and supplies. You may use them when it doesn't interfere with the campers. You'll have ample time to participate in all of these activities when you enter into them with the campers. Some camps also set aside a brief time each day for just the staff to use one facility.

As you work with your campers and observe other counselors, you'll notice that the wise counselor avoids personal arguments and emotional involvements with campers. Some campers find it difficult not to step out of bounds now and then, and you are the symbol of authority in their eyes.

They may even break a rule just to see how you will react! Correction should come quickly and quietly, and then the matter should be dropped.

Several rules or suggestions will help in establishing good relationships:

1. Have a genuine liking for people. If you don't please don't consider the field of counseling. You have to be interested in people and in finding their good points.

2. Be able to share with others—your knowledge, strength, relationship with God—everything that would help another individual.

3. Use the WE attitude—you're a cooperator. The camp is more interested in achieving its goals and objectives than in knowing who accomplished what! Be sure ideas are presented and the job is accomplished whether you get the credit or not.

4. Learn from your mistakes—profit from them and instead of calling them blunders or failures, consider them as an education. The difference between a successful and unsuccessful person is that the former doesn't make the same mistake twice.

5. Be decisive—don't wait too long to make decisions; have a sense of confidence.

6. Have some ability to compromise when the circumstances warrant it, but never compromise on camp standards and policies.

7. When you are wrong, admit it, and if you've made a mistake that affects others, apologize.

As you serve your church or camp as a counselor, and as you gain experience over the years, you will be given added responsibilities in your position. There will be occasions when you will have to reprimand and constructively criticize others. This may be campers or other counselors who work with and under your supervision. You'll need what has been called the peculiar ability to deal with others without giving offense—in other words, tact! When you must criticize, make sure that you criticize the act and not the person. This makes the individual feel less insecure and skeptical, and he finds it much easier to accept your advice. Never criticize when you are angry. If you let your emotions run away with your senses, your remarks will be regretted. Maintain and adopt a constructive attitude. Remember the purpose of criticism is to help others improve and do better. Criticism is an educational process, so make it constructive. Sarcasm has no place in criticism and will leave scars that take years to heal.

Whenever a mistake is made, it doesn't always mean that just one person was at fault. Someone else might be involved! Quite often others fail to carry out orders and duties because of faulty, unclear instructions, and perhaps you gave the instructions!

If you've ever been criticized in public, you know what a humiliating experience it is. One seems to lose his self respect and become bitter and resentful. Any and all criticism should come in private.

A final suggestion has been labeled the "sandwich" method of criticism. This involves slipping your criticism or suggestions for improvement in between two layers of compliments. The compliments should be sincere and if so, you'll find a receptive listener.

Suggestions and more suggestions on how to work with others—and yet how important it is that you be able to work well hand in hand with people. The finest suggestions, helps and admonitions were penned by Paul, the apostle. "Be humble and gentle. Be patient with each other, making allowance for each other's faults because of your love. Try always to be led along together by the Holy Spirit, and so be at peace with one another. We are all parts of one body, we have the same Spirit, and we have all been called to the same glorious future" (Ephesians 4:2-4).

"Don't use bad language. Say only what is good and helpful to those you are talking to, and what will give them a blessing. Don't cause the Holy Spirit sorrow by the way you live. Remember, He is the one who marks you present on that day when salvation from sin will be complete. Stop being mean, bad-tempered and angry. Quarreling, harsh words, and dislike of others should have no place in your lives. Instead, be kind to each other, tenderhearted, forgiving one another, just as God has forgiven you because you belong to Christ" (Ephesians 4:29-32).

"In everything you do, stay away from complaining and arguing" (Philippians 2:14).

"You are living a brand new kind of life that is ever learning more and more of what is right, and trying to be more and more like Christ Who created this new life within you. In this new life, one's nationality or race or education or social position is unimportant. Such things mean nothing; whether a person has Christ is what matters, and He is equally available to all. Since you have been chosen by God Who has given you a new kind of life, and because of His deep love and concern for you, you should practice tenderhearted pity and kindness to others. Don't worry about making a good impression on them but be ready to suffer quietly and patiently. Be gentle and ready to forgive; never hold grudges. Remember, the Lord forgave you, so you must forgive others. Most of all, let love guide your life for then the whole church will stay together in perfect harmony. Let the peace of heart which comes from Christ be always present in your hearts and lives, for this is your responsibility and privilege as members of His body. And always be thankful. Remember what Christ taught and let His words enrich your lives and make you wise; teach them to each other and sing them out in psalms and hymns and spiritual songs, singing to the Lord with thankful hearts" (Colossians 3:10-16).

"Living Letters"

Why's He Like That?

Chapter 4

JUNIOR AGE CAMPER—Ages 9-11

PHYSICALLY The junior-age child is a bundle of energy. He is very active and just loves to do things. He doesn't walk from place to place—he runs. He plays, wrestles, dives around the room or play area and is constantly on the go. DO is the word for the junior. He is strong and healthy at this age, and the susceptibility of early childhood is passing. The smaller muscles are developing. He still needs proper food, rest and supervision. The growth rate is slowed and he is beginning to fill out. Girls at this age are sometimes taller than the fellows. He really loves the out of doors and doesn't like to feel penned in. This is the time of adventure and hiking, horseback riding, hunting, fishing. He likes the difficult and competitive and notices the accomplishments of others. If he is interested enough, and challenged, he will practice constantly to accomplish his goal. He has the tendency to make a sharp distinction between work and play.

Suggestions: Provide a variety of constructive things for him to do. Let him choose those that appeal to him the most. Develop leadership ability and responsibility by structuring and providing the proper training situations for him. Challenge his ability with projects and games. Make a game out of the work projects. Do things with him and not for him. You need to be aware of the individual who tires easily, and see to it that he gets enough sleep and relaxation.

Because he admires strength and power, you can show him how God enabled men and women in the Bible to be strong and to do his will. Show how he, too, can be strong in his own Christian life.

MENTALLY At this stage he has many interests. Anything new holds a fascination for him. He is inquisitive and wants to know "why" and what makes things tick. He likes to read and he may not be too selective in his reading material. He enjoys history and geography and is developing a great interest in facts. His ability to memorize is very sharp and he has great capacity for retention. He's a collector and keeps things because of the material itself, or for some future use.

This is an age of realism and he enjoys real life stories. His imaginative play decreases the older he becomes. He is an imitator. He is able to draw general conclusions and is beginning to note relationships. He is beginning to understand how things and events fit together. At times, he can be quick to jump to conclusions and care must be exercised to point out all sides to him. His attention span is lengthening and can be from 20-40 minutes. Sometimes he can be interested in a project for an entire day, but when he drops it, he sometimes drops it completely.

Suggestions: Capitalize on his wide variety of interests and encourage him to ask questions. Help and lead him to answer some of his own questions. This can be the ideal time to stimulate his desire to know God and his plan of salvation. This is the age to teach him about the chronology, history and geography of the Bible and God's wonderful creation.

His collecting ability can be a source of enjoyment, not only to himself, but to others, and there are many objects at camp that could be used to help him begin a hobby.

His curiosity and "why" attitude can be directed to discover why people act the way they do and how God deals with them. This can lead into a discussion of his own relationship with Christ.

Help him to acquire good reading material, especially when he returns home. Christian fiction, biography, Bible storybooks, and especially the Bible itself are materials which he needs. You may have a library or bookstore at camp and your guidance here may instill some values of selection for future reference. Present the Scripture as the Word of God. Deal with some of his problems while at camp and show him the answers. This will help him to continue reading the Bible and memorize many passages that will further help him.

SOCIALLY AND EMOTIONALLY He can accept some responsibility, but he doesn't like authority over him. He is striving to become more independent. BUT he does respect authority and wants limits. The gang stage is present here and the leadership within the gang shifts according to the activity. His friends are sought out from within his own age group and he favors his own sex.

Within the past few years, the junior age has been paying more attention to the opposite sex than before and in some communities and schools, dating activities at this age are even encouraged! From this, we occasionally run into a youngster who is quite interested in the opposite sex. For the most part, however, there still exists some good natured antagonism between boys and girls. The boys naturally think of themselves as being bigger, braver and stronger.

The junior is very proud of any newly acquired skills and lacks patience with a younger child who can't do as he can. Teamwork is important and so are contests. Ball games and any competition are the vogue for these youngsters. They are hero worshipers now, and also very conscious of their own abilities and enjoy telling about past deeds and exploits. Fairness and honesty are concerns and they usually give in proportion to what they receive. Any recognition that they can elicit from you is gratifying.

Their frankness may sometimes surprise you. Be alert to discern the truth in what they tell, as exaggeration can be very common. The traits that children criticize most in others are attention-getting behavior, fighting, bossiness, being grouchy, and not being helpful to others.

Emotionally, they have just a few fears at this age but the present-day pressures are ever increasing. There are pressures from society, the threat of all-out war, the continual barrage of advertising, and the desire to succeed academically and socially. All of these have increased over the years, and the effect can be evidenced in some of the distorted and disrupted lives you find. Knowing the environmental background of your campers will aid you in your counsel. Quick temper is a problem; they tend to flare up in a moment's notice. Any outward displays of affection are generally repulsed, especially by the boys. A well-developed sense of humor characterizes this group and adds to the delightfulness of working with them.

Suggestion: He will respond to you much more if you act as a guide and not a dictator. When you present plans, do it enthusiastically and use the "let's do" approach. If he can see the advantages of complete participation and cooperation, he will go along with it. He will participate if he feels that he is cooperating rather than submitting. He can be challenged to use his leadership ability for God right here at camp, and then at home and school. If he realizes that it is a rewarding experience to serve God in a wholehearted manner, he will. Camp projects and activities that require teamwork and competition will be satisfying. Structure projects and games so that he is able to achieve satisfying results. He becomes discouraged by failure. Scripture can be used to show how a Christian acts and should act toward others, and how to become an effective witness.

The junior's desire to achieve can be directed toward the areas of Bible memorization, helping around the camp and participation in camp services and camp fires. He may find it easy to live the Christian life here at camp, but you will have to challenge and prepare him to live for Christ when he returns home. Give him specific examples of what he can do for and with others. Capitalize on his hero worship stage to provide ample opportunity to give him Christian heroes to look up to and to emulate. Well-known Christians in various fields, such as science, sports, school and missionary work will show him that Christians can be outstanding, and have wonderful opportunities in their vocation. Heroes from the Old and New Testament should be among those that he seeks after. Jesus Christ should be at the center of his life, as far as following any one person is concerned! It is also true that your own example will speak louder than anything you happen to say.

Opportunity for developing sportsmanship is an area that will be a challenge. He plays and competes to win and often finds it hard to accept failure and defeat. Help him to face this and to learn to derive the value out of an activity without having to win to receive any benefit.

Any fears that he may have can be discussed and evaluated. There are some things to fear and there are other fears that are unfounded. Here, as everywhere else, the Scriptures should be presented.

SPIRITUALLY It is very difficult to distinguish spiritual characteristics from the others; the spiritual area of a person's life cannot be divorced from the other aspects. Many applications have already been made to this, but a few facts here may complete the picture. A junior-age camper can understand Bible doctrine now and knows what sin and salvation are. In fact, this is one of the peak ages for commitments to Christ. Naturally, a real effort should be made to present to him the person of Jesus Christ, who is able to take away all sin. The junior doesn't completely grasp symbolism and doesn't really appreciate it, either. Object lessons at camp should be selected carefully, or he will never get the point.

He will raise real and pertinent questions about Christianity, and your answers should be truthful and scripturally based. If you don't know the answer, admit it and attempt to find out. Standards can be high and you can help him to meet them, but be sure the standards are realistic. He needs Biblical principles on which to base his actions. Whatever you do, avoid emotional appeals in presenting Christ to this age group.

JUNIOR HIGH CAMPER–Ages 12-14

This age has been labeled the "mixed-up" age, or

the "time of turbulence," or yet the "goof-off" stage. No matter what you call it, it is an age of transition.

PHYSICALLY This is the person who readily responds to action. This is a period of rapid, and sometimes uneven growth with an abundance of energy. He may appear to be as strong (and some as big!) as an adult, but awkward as a new-born colt. The junior high feels increased energy and strength, but hates to admit that he is tired or that he should slow his pace. Girls physically are ahead of the boys. This is the time of puberty, and there are definite physical changes taking place in both sexes.

Suggestions: As his counselor, you are responsible for him; even in matters of proper food, rest and exercise. Participation in games that allow him to use most of his muscles are best, but he also needs direction to some of the less energetic activities at camp, such as crafts. This is an important time for establishing principles of proper care of one's body, and to realize that God created man in this way for a particular purpose. He can realize that his body is a temple of the Holy Spirit, and he needs to care for and govern it according to the way that God has set forth. Activities and habits that are harmful to the physical growth of a person, such as drugs, tobacco and alcohol, can be discussed in the light of the Scriptures.

You can be sure that he will have many questions concerning some of the changes that are taking place in his body.

MENTALLY At this time, the junior high camper is nearing the adult level of mental capacity. There is a greater ability to exercise reason and judgment, and he will if given the proper conditions and opportunity. He likes to use his imagination and investigate. If real life is lacking and dissatisfying, he can retreat into a world of fantasy and satisfy his needs somewhat in this manner. However, if life can be made enjoyable and meaningful enough for him, this is a much more suitable alternative. He is alert and delights in competition. Quizzes and the opportunity to grapple with thought problems can be a real challenge to him now.

Verbalized criticism is a byword with him, as he voices his likes and dislikes very adamantly. This, however, is generally balanced with a good sense of humor.

Suggestions: Stimulate his thinking to wider areas and guide his verbal expression. He needs reasons for doing things. Teach him to base his decisions on fact and not emotion. This will assist him to weather some difficult moments.

Present the Scriptures in such a way that he finds the meaning and answers for himself. Present them in a practical daily-related manner. If the truths are vital and pertinent to his needs and problems, and he sees the value and profit from the Scripture, he will grasp hold and be challenged to a personal Bible study.

Because he is so critical and judgmental, he can be assisted to see that there is a standard by which he can judge and make discernments, and this standard is in the Scriptures. He will still need your help in solving some of his problems, so don't leave him to his own resources too quickly.

SOCIALLY The adolescent is a social creature —this is so true! In some ways, he becomes more preoccupied with social activities the older he becomes. The younger teen likes gang or team activities, but the ninth grader is more interested in social contacts and parties, and resents the younger teenagers. Even with the interest in social contacts, there are many adjustments to make at this time, and the problems that arise seem to dominate his entire life and affect everything that he does! Studies in school may falter during this period as this other interest has precedence now.

Both boys and girls now have more interest in one another and there is increased dating and going steady with this age group. Girls mature ahead of the boys and become interested in the opposite sex about a year in advance of the boys. They sometimes give the appearance of being more aggressive in their social contacts. They also prefer to date older boys.

Group activities are very popular now. In addition, the junior high feels less conspicuous and more comfortable or safe in this situation. Clowning around and showing off is a very normal process for him.

He has a strong desire to be treated as an "adult" and not as a child. Adult restraints are cast aside, or at least he attempts to cast them aside. The desire of an individual is strong and any type of control by adults or exercise of authority may be resisted or resented.

Suggestions: Group activities are essential now

and some young people will have to be taught to be a part of a group and how to act within the group setting. Mixer games, or activities that enable campers to get to know one another right away help create a healthier atmosphere socially.

In his group Bible study he likes to discuss and express his own doubt, feelings, thoughts and applications. These discussions are very popular and helpful if handled correctly. He needs an atmosphere that doesn't draw too much attention to him. Show him how Christ can help him in his new adjustment problems and how God cares for any and all problems. The Scripture also gives fellows and girls guidelines for behavior and how to get along with others. The teachings of Paul in the epistles can be very applicable here. If the campers can use the teachings while at camp and experience the satisfaction of achieving better relations by living according to the Scriptures, then you have been a real counselor and a teacher.

This is the opportunity to challenge him to use his social contacts and involvement for witnessing. This can begin while at camp with some of the non-Christian youth and can carry over when he returns to his community.

Don't be surprised if you get a negative reaction at first. You represent authority to him. In time, by being friendly and fair, good rapport can be established. He needs someone to confide in now and you are the most likely candidate. Your guidance and lack of bossiness in your dealings with him will pay rich dividends. By opening up to you and admiring you he gives you the opportunity for presenting Jesus Christ and the Christian life.

Now that he is seeking independence, assist him in seeing that when one becomes independent, he also assumes more responsibilities. The responsible person is one who shows that he is capable of growing up and deserves independence. Some rules are necessary and most of them are for our own protection and security. Point out that the guidelines and pattern for living in the Scripture enable him to really live life and get the most from life. If he sees these principles in action in your life, and finds that they really work, then he will follow you and grasp the Scriptures as his guide.

EMOTIONALLY This is a trying time and one of upheaval. Frustration, new and uncontrolled emotions, impulsiveness, uncertainty—all these characterize the young adolescent. Don't attempt to predict what he will do or say, he is unpredictable. This is involved in his thrust for independence. He finds it difficult to make the transition from childhood to adolescence, and he lacks confidence. He can't be sure of himself, nor the reactions of others to him. Acceptance is very important, particularly with his own peer group. The opinion of adults does count, too. Because of his uncertainty, he sometimes is willing to try just about anything. Much of this is due to the fact that he really doesn't know what he wants. His imagination can be vivid and his outward emotions or reactions may be the opposite of what he's really feeling. He seeks to shield his true feelings.

Suggestions: Patience, understanding and love will heal many of the torments that he experiences.

If you expect adult or older adolescent behavior from him, you'll be disappointed. Respect him for what he is and work with him. Help him feel wanted and respected. Help him to set some standards for himself and assist him to live up to them. Goals can be set now that will add stability to his life.

Your interest and concern will mean much to him and will pave the way for the presentation of God's love, acceptance and provision. Then he will find that in Christ, he is a new creature. If he can put Christ first in his life, the other things will be put in their proper place. He's looking for a way of life that is acceptable and you can point him to the Christian life. Always stay with a newborn Christian. The Christian life just doesn't happen, but must be nurtured, cultivated, and weeded before you can expect to see indications of a harvest. This camper needs you to teach him the way of the Lord.

SPIRITUALLY This can be a time of spiritual awakening as well as a time of doubts. All questions should be dealt with honestly and scripturally. Let him ask his questions and answer them. His spiritual development will depend upon his church background, Bible knowledge, and comprehension. This is another age in which many make decisions for Christ, but the appeal must not be made on the basis of emotion. All Bible study must be relevant and directed toward his needs.

He can derive satisfaction from the Scriptures and from a time of personal study. Some of the newer versions make this a much more meaningful experience, and it's the wise counselor who goes prepared with several good versions of the Bible. Prayer will be very personal and self-directed at this time, but he can learn to be concerned for others: friends at camp, non-Christian friends at home, family, the church, missionaries, the camp. As he hears your concern and love reflected in your prayers for and with him, he will sense the meaningful richness of a sincere prayer life, and he will find that his life will be different!

HIGH SCHOOL CAMPER—Ages 15-17

PHYSICALLY For most high school campers, this is the time of reaching physical maturity. As you watch this group consume food, you get the impression that they have been starved for weeks before descending upon your campgrounds. They abound in energy. Their coordination is being refined. They are mature sexually.

Suggestions: Camp activities should include a well-balanced athletic program that is suited to the needs of both girls and fellows, and gives them opportunity to get the necessary exercise. The high schooler needs to be encouraged to get proper rest. Encourage habits of proper care for his body. Remind him that his body is the temple of the Holy Spirit. You may need to give health instructions and discussions concerning the use of tobacco, drugs and alcohol. These topics are usually part of the discussion periods. Some high school students are already involved in their usage and others are wondering about them. Facts that you present must be valid and current, but the scriptural approach pointing out God's guidelines for one's life is your final authority.

MENTALLY High school students are characterized as sharp! Reasons are a must for him when you ask him to do or believe something. He questions constantly, and he has reached the peak of his ability to learn. He thinks logically, he investigates, evaluates and wants to make his own decisions. Arguments are common as he likes to think that he has the last word and is right. Because he is so close to adulthood, the drive for independence is very evident and the sense of being capable of handling his own affairs is prominent. Vocational interest is one of his major concerns as school and home are pressing him for a decision in order to guide and direct his future schooling. Imagination is vivid but he is concerned with reality.

Suggestions: A mental challenge is needed by this age group. A camp program that emphasizes the physical side with a lack in the mental area will create biblical illiterates. Let the young person express his views and questions, but study so you have at least some of the answers when asked. The Scripture can answer his questions about life. His mentality, as well as his vocational future, needs to come under the direction of God. His mental capabilities can be used for God, and he is capable of serious Bible study. Books and Bible study methods and materials can be of great service in order to help him continue his study when he returns to his home. As you talk with him, he will listen to you more if you respect and accept the fact that he is more independent and is moving closer to adulthood. Asking for his opinion or assistance and guidance, in place of bossing, will help to gain his acceptance. Show him how God has a plan for his life and has standards and rules for living which must be obeyed. Don't hesitate to challenge him with thought-provoking questions in your cabin devotions, but know when to remain quiet and let him speak and answer his own questions. Pray with him, as well as for him, and perhaps you will be able to show him how his prayers have been answered, even during the week of camp.

SOCIALLY Socially, the high school camper is gregarious. This is often one of the most important areas of his life, and he must be accepted by the right people, club and clique, or his world crumbles. Often he sacrifices his own values in order to be accepted. He cannot tolerate the feeling of being "left out." He has his own close group of associates. Parties are important outlets, fashions must be the latest, and amusements that provide thrills and action are part of this process known as the high school years. Going steady is very common and provides security. The area of sex poses many problems, and most high school students have conflicts over the extent of their sex behavior. Even those with strong moral standards have difficulty controlling this impulse. Boy-girl relationships sometimes dominate and control every area of his life, including his involvement in the church.

Suggestions: Help him feel accepted within the cabin and the entire camp community. Cliques should be avoided and campers should be encouraged to widen their social contacts. Attempt to draw those who are quiet and restrained into social activities and cabin discussions. It is very easy to respond favorably to the bright, outgoing socially aggressive person while ignoring the quiet, perhaps inhibited person, but the latter may need you more than the other. No matter what the case, don't favor any special one or group. The quiet one needs greater discrimination in the field of friendships and needs to develop judgment with reference to people. Help him to know that God accepts him, no matter who and what he is. When we respond to God's invitation, he responds even more greatly to us. All individuals can become something through Jesus Christ.

If you can suggest activities and opportunities for him to develop self-confidence in social situations, his total life adjustment will be more acceptable to him and to others. Counseling on boy and girl friend problems will consume a large portion of your time. Your own standards and patterns must be well established before you can guide in this area. You might let him know that you and the speakers are available for counseling on any area, including this one. Good Christian books can be presented and used while there at camp and your camp discussions may have a tendency to center around this topic. Be careful that all of your cabin devotions and discussion time isn't dominated totally by this topic since it is a favorite. The Scripture has a frank and thorough presentation about sex and its intended usage in the plan of God. Delve into the Scriptures and direct him to God's standard. Show how God can help him to govern his body.

EMOTIONALLY Emotions are still intense and fluctuating, but the high schooler is beginning to be more stable and dependable. He is sensitive and may keep his feelings to himself and attempt to conceal them. His needs range from security to thrills, and he is aware of how he appears and feels. He is planning for the future, but the future offers some uncertainty to him. He must consider marriage, college, work or the military.

Suggestions: This is the time when he needs to consider and appreciate others, as well as himself, and attempt to meet the needs of those about him. By realizing his importance to God, he can feel secure and accepted. He may need encouragement and assistance in considering what to do in the future. Perhaps you can help him to choose a school. If you lack experience and knowledge, guide him to someone who can help him. Now he can be challenged to life service in the area of Christian vocations. Work with him to discover God's will for his life through commitment, prayer and Bible study. Assist him to find healthy expressions and accepted ways of expressing his emotions.

SPIRITUALLY This can be a time of spiritual conflicts and doubts, but it can also be a time when there is a warm, personal faith. It is a period when many drop away from the church because of the influence of friends or the lack of a well-developed faith, or even more unfortunate, the church fails to reach them. Give the young person leadership in thinking through the great and important doctrines of the Christian faith. Dogmatism is disliked in others, but he will appreciate and accept the authority of the Scriptures if you honestly deal with his doubts. The faith of another Christian can have a stabilizing influence on him. Personal testimonies of other Christians he admires and respects will carry a lot of weight. The high school camper needs to have an active and expressive faith. Use him at camp. Motivate and utilize him in Christian service, or he may be lost to the church. He may look forward to counseling someday as a number of camps use older high school students as counselor trainees, or junior counselors.

Me, a Leader?

Chapter 5

PLACE: The craft hut at a Christian camp high in a mountain range
TIME: Afternoon during free time
SITUATION: A junior-age boy is struggling to construct an object with hammer, glue and nails. He hopes to finish this by the time camp is over so that he can take it home and give it to his parents. Hopefully, this is going to be a small bookcase with a Scripture verse burned into each side. He is having difficulty, though, as he is trying to nail the pieces together with nails that are too weak, so they are bending and not holding the wood together.

You are the counselor. How would you attempt to help him?

If your concept of leadership is the authoritarian type, you'll jump right in and say, "Here, I'll do that for you. You're doing it all wrong. Watch me and I'll show you how. You can't glue it that way and can't use nails that bend!" This is the authoritarian approach. Whether an individual is involved in a craft project or a group in a work and service project, this method operates on basically the same premise. The autocratic leader determines all policies and techniques. Even the activities are dictated. In work situations, only one step is mentioned at a time and members are uncertain of what is to come next.

This "leader" leads primarily by force and fear of consequences. He generally has an over-evaluation of himself so that he doesn't consider the opinions or suggestions of others. Some of his over-control policy stems from a lack of security on his part. No questioning of authority or methods is encouraged or permitted, and disobedience to the established rule usually brings certain punishment and reprimand.

For the most part, leaders such as this have difficulty controlling their tempers and they sometimes delight in bossing others. When work tasks are assigned, such as cleaning up the cabin or the campgrounds, these leaders pick who does what and with whom. Whenever praise or criticism is meted out, they are personal, but for the most part remain aloof from the rest of the group. Obedience and productivity are stressed. Basic respect and acceptance of individual importance is lacking. The authoritarian method accomplishes much as far as time is concerned, but it also creates varied reactions. Hostility, aggression and fear are very common. Some campers respond by complete and unhesitant obedience, whereas others begin to detest all types of authority and discipline.

Let's return to the camper who is having difficulty with the weak nails and his bookcase. If you believe in another type of leadership called the "laissez-faire," how will you approach this situation? Well, it will be completely the opposite of the authoritarian. You will give barely any help to our young struggling (and by this time, frustrated) camper. You will sit by, observe, and leave him to figure it out for himself. You favor almost complete freedom for a group or individual, with an absolute minimum of leader participation.

There are times when this leader makes it very clear that he will participate at the minimum level or often not at all. He feels that a group or person can develop self-reliance and learning experiences by practicing complete self-direction. He goes along with what the group suggests. The difficulty here is that many campers aren't ready or prepared for this loose structured situation and are disorganized, because of the lack of leadership. This approach presumes considerable strength and ability on the part of the group. Campers don't respect the lack of control and discipline on the part of the leader. They would prefer to have limits and some guidance. Very little work is accomplished with this approach.

For the last time, let's return to that craft hut where our young camper is being approached by another type of leader, you, the democratic counselor. As you approach, you perceive what has happened and comment, "It looks like that's going to be pretty wobbly. Do you have any idea why?" The camper thinks a minute and replies, "Well, I've been putting in all these nails but most of them bend and this thing wiggles all over. It looks like just two or three nails have gone through. Do you think these thicker nails would work better?" And you reply, "That just might do the trick. Why not try them, and if you like I'll hold the wood for you so it's steady." This is the democratic approach as it applies to the individual.

As it applies to the group, it means that all policies and decisions are a matter of total group involvement. The group discusses and decides and you encourage and assist. You really enjoy your campers. You know when to have a good time with them and when to exercise control and discipline.

In a way, this process is slower than the autocratic, as you need more time to discuss and plan, but it also means total involvement of the individuals of your group or cabin unit. You realize that it's better from your perspective to wait and let the group decide than to jump in and accomplish the task (probably in a more efficient manner and quicker, too). You help the group learn how to make decisions. There is free expression of opinions and feelings and individual differences are utilized. This approach usually results in satisfying interpersonal relations among the campers and counselor. It is not always the most efficient as far as work productivity is concerned in a short period of time. You assess and evaluate the requirements and needs of the situation and help the group to the greatest possible extent within any limitations that the group might have.

This type of leadership, as well as other methods, should be evaluated as there are some weaknesses. Don't leave the group so alone that they are unable to operate and so deteriorate into the laissez-faire method. Each group will react in a different manner, depending upon its constellation, so be ready to adjust and don't expect the next group to be like the last one. If the campers haven't had training in the democratic process, don't expect them to assume this type of decision making. You'll have to spend time in training them. On the other hand, don't become discouraged with a new group and assume that they are incapable of learning or will be unresponsive.

The question that you may have is, "Which method shall I use or shall I use all three?" Most camps favor the democratic method, but with the realization that it isn't always used in its purest form. Certain rules are fixed and have to be maintained. Your camp will probably suggest guidelines to use in your leadership approach. Some have attempted to alternate from one to another, depending upon the situation. However this changeable approach can lead to confusion and frustration on the part of the group. The democratic method (with variations, if necessary) has proved to be the best method.

HOW MUCH SHOULD A LEADER LEAD?

A leader makes use of his own natural ability. You may not have a thorough knowledge of leadership techniques, but if you're willing to learn and improve you are on the right track. The good leader anticipates situations and makes adequate preparation for them. If there is a lack of leadership at a particular moment, he senses this and fills the gap and does more than his share willingly. Good leadership does not impose adult standards on non-adult personalities. Teaching is accomplished by guidance and not bossiness. All groups and individuals make mistakes and learn by these mistakes.

These are the marks of a good leader:

1. He leads by example.
2. He has a good sense of humor and exercises it to avert crises and keep molehills from becoming mountains.
3. His thoughts are not inverted toward himself, but rather outwardly toward the greater "we."
4. He capitalizes on the power of suggestion and subtly plants ideas to sprout and grow. He leaves the group free to pick up the hint and proceed to enthusiastically carry it out, making it their own, improving and altering it as many minds go to work.
5. He tactfully avoids serious misunderstandings and feuds with others and sincerely attempts to see their side of the question. He realizes that if he once arouses another's antagonism, he has probably lost all chance to influence him in the future.

6. When there is work to be done, he is in the midst of it, sleeves rolled up and hands dirty.

7. He understands the force of group pressure and group opinion. He realizes that there is danger in letting campers entirely rule themselves. They still have immature judgment and can be cruel and go to extremes when judging each other.

8. He is mindful of the value of "fun," for happy campers seldom become problems. If he is teaching a new skill, he is thorough, but patient and understanding, and proceeds with an informal, friendly manner. He knows the value of a laugh and always has time for a good joke. He devises ways to make chores fun instead of irksome tasks.

9. He knows that campers, no matter how much they complain and grouse, do not really enjoy slovenly, careless standards of conduct. They soon lose respect for a leader who tolerates such laxness. He recognizes that a request gets better response than an order but that, when orders have been found necessary, they must be enforced.

10. He gives praise freely and can see good in nearly everything and everybody. He realizes that insincere or overused praise is quickly detected and discounted. He avoids nagging and excessive fussiness about detail.

11. He foresees an impending crisis and tries to avert it if he can. If Johnny is chanting how much he dislikes spinach, he does not wait until the whole table is lamenting their pet dislikes, but quietly introduces a new topic.

12. He shuns public scenes whenever possible. A "bawling out" before others hurts a camper's pride

and makes him react by (1) giving up, or (2) growing resentful and intent on revenge. He knows that emotional hurts are even more serious than physical ones. He gives the erring camper a chance to "save face" by seemingly ignoring his misdemeanor in public but later takes it up with him privately in a frank and friendly manner. He knows that "badness" often results from embarrassment or not knowing just what is the right thing to do. He rejects bad conduct but not the camper guilty of it.

13. He seldom tells a camper what to do, but instead, discusses the problem with him, drawing out the correct solution from him. He never sends a camper away dejected and hopeless but leaves him realizing that the counselor still has faith in him.

14. He never uses physical punishment. It seldom brings about the desired result, is usually against camp rules, and might involve him or the camp in legal difficulties.

15. He uses disciplinary measures sparingly. He must be convinced that they are in the best interests of the culprit and that he is not acting vindictively or in an effort to save his own pride. Punishment is so easy to administer and gets such quick and sure results (outwardly, at least) that it is often misused or overused. The superior counselor handles his group so skillfully that serious disciplinary problems seldom occur. However, sometimes the day comes when action can no longer be postponed. People are usually good sports about accepting punishment which is deserved and not based upon partiality and/or spite. When discipline is necessary, it should follow as closely as possible on

the heels of the misdemeanor and should bear some relationship to it if possible. For instance, depriving a camper of his dessert would be appropriate only for a dining room misdeed. Using work as a punitive measure belittles it and drags it down from the place of honor it ought to hold. However, it may be appropriate for a camper who has cluttered up the grounds, thrown food around the dining room, or otherwise created extra work for someone else.

16. He knows that people usually live up to what is expected of them and that the best way to get a camper to climb to new heights is to show that he expects him to do just that. Issuing a challenge is a very potent force.

17. He does not take a camper's bad conduct as a personal affront. He realizes that it is more likely to be a reaction from a past experience or an outside worry. A camper's rebellion at even a reasonable amount of discipline may be caused by having had too much of it at home or school.

18. He satisfies his own basic desires in a healthy way. For instance, he does not secure needed affection by encouraging an unhealthy attachment from a camper. He does not unduly encourage campers to bear tales or slavishly serve him.

19. He seldom bursts forth in momentary anger but instead waits through a "cooling off" period to get the facts and consider all angles so that he can approach it with a cool head and sound judgment.*

When one speaks of motivation and control, the

*From Mitchell and Crawford: *Camp Counseling*, 3rd edition. Philadelphia, W. B. Saunders Co., 1961. Pages 84-86.

word discipline generally is raised. The word discipline comes from the same Greek word as "disciple," and basically, the disciples were learners or pupils. Discipline is learning or a process by which people learn what is acceptable, desirable and pleasant for all.

There are a number of specific behavior problems that arise, and each problem generally has a specific cause.

Why do campers behave in such varied ways? Many have needs that are unsatisfied, and in their attempt to satisfy these, they behave in a socially unacceptable manner. Some are seeking attention or attempting to demonstrate their power. Others have a strong compelling force or drive to punish others or get even with them for something, either real or imagined. Yet, there are those who feel and act inadequate, and they demonstrate their inadequacy. This doesn't mean that the goal or reason is a constant one, for the motivating force behind an action may be different on each occasion.

Do you feel that undisciplined behavior is something that the camper willingly seeks to relinquish? Not necessarily, as this behavior can be very satisfying to him. Basically, most individuals give up a satisfaction only for a substitute that is more satisfying. If your discipline is going to be effective, you need to know what the camper's actions do for him; what he receives from them and how satisfying the reward is to him. Determine his unfulfilled needs and attempt to meet them. They could be needs that should have been met many years before and you'll just scratch the surface as you attempt to work with him.

Don't expect too much if you have a serious problem, others may have tried to handle it before you with no success. Discipline, too, is a process and takes thought, perception, time and prayer. If you consider discipline just an emergency measure, the so-called results that you achieve won't be permanent. Little, if any, learning will have taken place.

HOW TO GET THEM STARTED

Controlling and motivating a group of enthusiastic campers can present a challenge to even the most experienced counselor and camp worker. There are always several answers to a discipline or motivational problem, and these answers may be right or wrong at a given time. The kind of discipline you use will have to be directly related to the specific goal you have in mind. The devices mentioned are the ones that are the most frequently used. Some are effective and others are quite poor. The poorer ones are presented to show some of the possible results.

Just picture yourself settling down in your cabin with your campers all tucked into their bunks and ready to go to sleep. You are unable to get to sleep because one of the fellows is an incessant talker and refuses to settle down and be quiet. He whispers, laughs, throws candy at others at the other end of the cabin and just won't cooperate and quiet down. How will you solve this? How will you deal with him? Some of the methods that have been tried are as follows:

1. "Because-I-said-so" technique: This is done by going to the boy and stating, "I simply won't have my sleep and the sleep of the other campers disturbed by your messing around. I just won't tolerate this!" What you've done here is to make yourself the object against which his misbehavior is now directed. If he has a desire to please you, he'll be quiet, but if he wants to react to you and keep you riled, he'll continue his actions. This has now become a personal involvement between two individuals and even a power struggle between you. Before, it was simply a matter of not settling down and going to sleep. Don't use yourself as the final authority or indicate that this is going to be a struggle between the camper and you.

2. "Think-about-it-this-way" approach: Here we have the same situation, but approach it in the manner of, "Well, it looks like you really aren't sleepy yet. What do you think the results might be if you don't get your sleep tonight and keep others awake at the same time?" This is putting the responsibility back on to the camper and assists him to come to the proper solution. You may have to rephrase the question and ask it several times befor he'll settle down enough to give a serious answer. But when he does, you'll have the opportunity to agree with his solutions and even reinforce and reinterpret them to him.

Helping campers to sense and predict the logical consequences of an act can develop into a learning experience about life that can be applied to many areas. Sometimes individuals have to experience the natural consequences of an action before the lesson is fully learned. Natural consequences represent the pressure of real life. This may be all right as long as there is no injury to people or damage to camp property. You may have a camper who can never be on time for the daily horseback riding. You tell him that he'll miss his ride if he is late, but you always hold up everyone else until this boy comes trooping down to the stable. If he had to experience the logical consequence of missing his ride for a day, he wouldn't be late the next time!

Research and practical study has indicated that letting children and teenagers experience the natural consequences of their misbehavior is a very important factor in maintaining order. Correct behavior and adherence to rules arise from within when this method is implemented. The person soon realizes that it is more satisfying to respect rules and regulations than it is to break them.

This method does not demand any submission to another person, either! However, all too often counselors either become too impatient with this method or moved out of pity, give in and thus break down everything that they have worked toward. You are teaching respect for order, rules and are helping to develop conformity. The camper experiences the natural consequences of his action, and not the punishment or penalty administered by someone other than himself. Consequences are a natural result of breaking the rules. Place the responsibility for changing the situation up to the person involved.

This method will break down if the tone of your voice or implication gives the impression that what is happening is punishment. One summer, this incident was observed. The rule of the camp was that all campers had to be in the dining hall on time and anyone arriving more than ten minutes late would have to miss that meal. Several campers developed the habit of coming in eight or nine minutes late each time and it wasn't long before their calculations were off and they arrived at the dining hall too late. One of the counselors wanted to let them come ahead and eat. He felt that it would be cruel to make them go hungry for the afternoon. The camp director, however, handled the situation in a way that produced results. He approached the campers and mentioned that he was sorry that they had arrived too late, but that the rules of camp had been explained to everyone and anyone arriving late would have to miss the meal. Since they had chosen to be late, they had also made the choice of missing the meal. If they would like to eat the next meal, they would certainly be welcome to do so if they were there on time. You can imagine the results. When dinner time rolled around, the first in line were the hungry fellows, and from then on they were there on time. It was left up to the campers to change the situation.

3. "I-only-like-the-good-kids" threat: This is often used by the improperly trained counselor and is one which is most ineffective. This counselor, in approaching the sleepless camper problem says, "Now look, it's late and we want to get our sleep, and I really like kids who are quiet and conform to the rules. Now if you want me to like you, BE QUIET!" Or "If you continue to disturb us, you

might as well forget me as your friend. I don't care for campers who don't follow orders." Neither of these so-called techniques is very convincing.

4. "That's-Very-Good" opening: People respond quite favorably to praise and compliments, when they are used honestly and in proper proportion with other comments. Some campers can become dependent upon your words of praise. Some never experience commendation in their homes. Their day can be made or broken by the amount of praise that you give. People who are praised are usually inclined to continue in the action or behavior that won recognition. Be certain this is not flattery or verbal bribery. It will be obvious if it is.

5. "Do-It-Or-Else" method: When tempers begin to rise and everything else that you have tried seems to fail, then it is a temptation to attempt to gain control by making threats. Threats usually bring only momentary results. The most frequent types of threats are: Threats or appeals to morals—"Nice boys or girls never do anything like that." Age status—"Hey, there, you're not ten years old, you're fourteen, so why not act like it. Big kids don't do that sort of thing around this camp." Sex status—"Don't be a sissy, all the other fellows took an early morning dip. Aren't you a man yet?" Parental control—"Say, if you can't learn to conform, I'm just going to have to write your folks and we'll see what they have to say about this kind of thing." Higher authority—"Do it just one more time and I'm taking you to the girl's dean and then you'll really get it."

The use of any kind of higher authority in the camp can be functional if used in a non-threatening manner. Only as a last resort should you go to the camp director with a behavior problem, and be careful not to make the camp dean or director a "boogie man." All camps have some basic rules and standards and this can be the final source of authority, instead of blaming a person. The director and dean can aid in enforcing these rules, but to use them as a threat is unfair to them. You may limit their effectiveness in doing personal work with the campers by prejudicing the campers. Never use a threat which you don't intend to carry out.

Group Status—"How do you think the others are going to feel about you if you continue to act like this?" This method has proved effective if used and presented in a way that will be acceptable to the problem camper.

The inflection of your voice is so very important as you attempt to motivate and guide others. It might not be what you say but the way you say it that determines the outcome.

Methods which should not be used are ridiculing or using sarcasm or shaming, offering bribes, causing fear, or ignoring the person and acting as though he were not present. Now and then, these may seem to solve the problem for the moment, but what other and more serious problems are they helping to create? Discipline which the person does not understand, and cruelty in any physical or mental form should not be used.

Many of the suggestions mentioned so far are the type that camps prefer to have left at home. They have no place in proper leadership and motivation, but there are some that can be extremely effective.

1. Asking for individual or group evaluation. "What do YOU think of that?" Showing that you're interested in his reaction and opinion enlists his cooperation in what is important at that particular moment. Sometimes it helps to talk over the rules and get his reactions and ideas for behavior and suggestions on what to do when there is a rule infraction. You can use your skill to make the group members more secure. This will promote better group discipline through cooperative action.

2. Putting the choice in his hands with acceptance of the consequences. "Well Jim, it seems that we have a situation here in which you have a choice. You can either follow the rules like the rest of the guys and remain here at the swimming pool, or you can continue to break the rules and relinquish your swimming privileges for the next couple of days. Now you make the choice. If you decide to obey, fine. If you break the rules, then you've chosen to leave." This has proved to be a very effective method as the camper realizes that he is directly responsible for his behavior and the reaction to it. He can't blame anyone but himself if certain restrictions come about because of deviations from the rules.

3. Showing enthusiasm. "Hey, let's try this. It looks like a lot of fun."

4. Offering suggestions and explanations. "Why not try it this way?"

5. Posing a problem. Even though you may have the answer to a problem, let him have the fun of thinking it through and at the same time capture his attention and direction.

6. Pointing out alternatives. "It looks as though we could approach this in several ways. Why not give this method a try first?"

7. Asking the group to look at itself to see progress. "How are we doing?"

8. Suggesting resources. "Maybe the craft director could give us a hand here?"

9. Taking pride in his group. This develops group unity, spirit, and allegiance to you, your suggestions, and requests. Not orders! Use the term "we," not "I." Use the word "let's." If the camper likes you and respects you as a counselor, you won't need to motivate. If you want him to be disciplined, he must see a disciplined leader. He'll follow! Varying activities and keeping him busy will achieve wonders.

Remember, discipline or control is worthless unless it does more than just stop poor behavior. Effective discipline is directed toward the underlying sources of the difficulty, not toward the symptoms. It looks toward the future and is not so concerned with the past.

If you are angry—wait, and collect your wits and your feelings before you proceed. Be sure you are right, then proceed with fairness. Firmness is not measured by loudness. Avoid false accusations and don't jump to conclusions. Commands should be minimal and don't be a "picky" counselor, be concerned with major, but not minor issues. If you make a mistake or a goof, be able to laugh at yourself with the kids.

As you approach a loaded situation and a crisis is impending—proceed with caution. Kids think it is fun to get a counselor "riled up." Are you certain that when you have established discipline or control with a group, it is really discipline, or just outward temporary conformity, there IS a difference.

What Do I Say Next?

Chapter 6

Counseling is a relationship in which one person tries to help another to understand and solve problems. It is an understanding between persons which results in a change. It sometimes involves advice-giving, information-giving, interpretation of situations, encouraging the other person to think out or work out his difficulties and often, it involves just listening. Basically, it is a communication process. He speaks to you and you respond to him.

Christian counseling is unique because in the final analysis your counseling will lead to Christ. Your final source of authority is the Scripture.

Christian counseling goes beyond ordinary counseling. It supplies the answer for every problem in the person of Jesus Christ, and an authoritative guide for conduct in the Word of God. Therefore, your counseling has a deeper function—that of training a girl or boy to relate every aspect of life to Christ and look to him each moment.

There are many practical considerations. Camping may be an entirely new situation for some of your campers. You may not know him and he doesn't know you. The better you become acquainted, the more opportunities will be presented for you to counsel with him. You may have ten campers but don't think of them as just a group of boys or a group of girls—each is an individual and you need to think of him as such. Learning his name the very first day will make your job that much easier.

You may have some who will reject you. No matter how hard you try, there won't seem to be any breakthrough. Don't try to force yourself on him—all people are different. One camper may open up to you the first day. Another may wait until an hour before he leaves camp. People respond at different times and for different reasons.

The home backgrounds and environments from which campers come vary tremendously. Many come from homes in which there is division, separation and divorce. Some may not have a father or mother at home. For a weekend or week, you may be filling that need. Others come from homes in which the family is entrenched in the church program and the children may fit into camp. Or, they may be very rebellious. Be sympathetic toward all, no matter what the backgrounds. Try to understand each camper in the light of his environmental background and present status.

Don't assume at the beginning of the camp that you have some campers who have no difficulties at all. Some may not, but you have to know them well before this assumption can be made. Quite often the quiet model child has more problems than the boisterous cut-ups in your dorm. All behavior has significance.

As you show that you have a personal concern for each one and attempt to get close to him, openings will present themselves. Without prying, learn everything you can about each camper—age, interests, hobbies, position in family, social status, church backgrounds, camping experience, etc. To be a counselor, you have to be perceptive enough to realize when something is going on in the life of a child or adolescent. Often, just one word at the right time is all that is necessary to provide the opportunity to help him.

Be sensitive to the camper who may be trying to establish a contact with you. It could be someone in your own cabin or in someone else's group. If you notice that someone seems to hang back after a meeting or activity or even stays to help you do something in the dorm, this may be the time. Occasionally, he will begin with a question and ask your opinion. In doing this, he may be testing you to see if you're an accepting type of person and if you'll be willing to listen to any type of problem. Some have been known to begin by saying, "Hey,

I've got this friend of mine back home and the other day, he and his dad got into this row over how much money he was spending on himself. He thinks that his kid should help on the expenses of the car. What do you think about this and what could I tell my buddy?" Later, as you talk with him, you may find out that he is this so-called friend! He was hesitant to mention this at the beginning as he didn't know what type of reception he would receive.

Your availability will be an important factor in any counseling that you will do at camp. If the campers find you ready and willing to listen, they will seek you out. Don't appear so busy, rushed, or so important that they feel that they are bothering you. You are there at camp to work with them and don't let anything else interfere with your time that is devoted to them. If a counseling opportunity arises, "after swimming" or "after lunch" may be too late and the opportunity may be gone.

When people talk to you, do you listen? Can you determine what they are really saying, and do you appear interested? Do you wait to hear all of their story before you give your advice? If so, then you're doing the right thing. Many times, through the process of "talking it out" a person will be able to find the solution himself without your actually having told him. This happens if you're a good listener! In order for campers to fully express themselves, they must have your undivided attention. Know when to remain silent. Many a person has curtailed a camper's desire to talk by talking too soon and too much.

Are you able to talk with them on their own level? If so, there will be communication and it will be two-way. Terms and phrases that are ambiguous and foreign to a camper will just confuse and confound the problem. Biblical terms, such as "saved" and "born again" and "convicted" may mean a great deal to you, but what does it mean to the young person who lacks a biblical background? When you mention "saved," he might think that you're talking about being saved in the swimming pool. "Convicted" might mean guilty of a crime in a court! Use words he will understand and if you use a biblical phrase, explain it to him.

Know up-to-date terms and the current vocabulary of the age group with which you are working. This doesn't mean that you always have to use their "slang." You'll feel uncomfortable if the words are not a part of your own vocabulary. A good rule to follow is to use known terms to explain the unknown.

A positive attitude on your part, rather than a dogmatic approach, will help your counseling to be accepted. The only area that you can be dogmatic about is the vital, major area of biblical teaching. Amusements and areas connected with them can lead to difficulty. There will be various feelings and views represented, depending upon the camp, churches and denominations attending. An argumentative spirit in a counselor is a hindrance. If you present a positive picture of Christianity as evidenced by your daily life, others will want what you have.

How shock proof are you? Do you gasp or turn

red when you hear of the past exploits that your camper is relating to you? Try not to be amazed and excited when you learn of some of the past and present deeds. This only helps to reinforce to him that perhaps what he did was quite an event! Maintain your normal appearance and attempt to help him by putting him at ease. One of the better methods of doing this, especially if the individual is deeply concerned over the problem, is the fact that many others have faced the same problem and have been able to conquer it.

How do you react to a person who seems to have the answer for everything, even questions and problems out of his realm of knowledge? If your reaction is typical, you usually find out that this type of person isn't worth talking to. He doesn't know as much as he thinks he does. When you don't have the answer to a situation, don't pretend to have one. If you say that you do and the suggestions you give are later found to be invalid, then you've destroyed a counseling relationship. You are not a psychologist, nor a therapist, but you will still have to cope with problems. Thus, know your abilities and limitations and know when to seek assistance. Be honest and admit that you do have limitations and don't always have the answer. But show that you're willing to try to find the answer, or you'll attempt with his permission to help him find someone who is able to assist him. Perhaps one of the conference deans or speakers can be of assistance here.

When you are counseling with a child or youth concerning his personal problems, your goal is insight on his part which eventually arrives at a solution. The insight that you seek in counseling is that which enables a person to understand his own feelings, attitudes, and even motivation in order to discover the reason or basis for his problem.

Quite often, the problems brought to you are the result of faulty attitudes. External behavior is important, but more vital than that is the feeling or attitude. Jesus was insistent on the necessity of correcting inner attitudes. "But those things which proceed out of the mouth come forth from the heart; and they defile the man. For out of the heart proceed evil thoughts, murders, adulteries, fornications, thefts, false witness, blasphemies" (Matthew 15:18,19). When the inner attitudes are changed or modified, then new patterns of behavior come into being. This will come gradually as the two of you work together.

In addition, discovering the consequences of these in one's life will hasten the process of insight. The final phase is discovering the changes that he can make in his life to alleviate that which has been a hindrance. Often, the changes to be made are within himself, but at times those about him are the cause of the difficulty. It could be parents, siblings, friends, school, church, or even the other campers. Then a camper needs to learn how to adjust and work with the situation.

Your final overall goal in counseling is to lead the person (when ready) to Jesus Christ and to the rich and full life that knowing him can provide. You are not just after decisions, but lives that are changed because they have come face to face with Jesus

Christ and have accepted him as Lord, Saviour and Master of their lives.

BUT I WOULDN'T KNOW WHAT TO SAY!

When you counsel with individuals, be certain you are in a location where you have privacy and he isn't fearful that someone else is listening. Never reveal to other campers what has been told to you in confidence. If this happens, he won't confide in you again. Don't appear anxious or overly concerned as he talks to you. If he is hesitant to express himself, don't start by talking about his problem. Talk about an unemotional subject, one that will put him at ease and allay any fears he has. Try to say those things which will encourage him to continue talking.

What are some practical, yet simple techniques that you can use? What do you say? Asking questions can be of great help in aiding a person to verbalize his problems or thoughts. There are several types of questions that can be used.

1. Information-gaining questions. There are times when you need to have more facts or perhaps you've forgotten some of the details that the person has mentioned. Ask for necessary and specific information—about persons, things or occurrences. Sometimes the camper talks as though he thought that you realized and understood everything about him when you don't. Example: "Which sister was that?" "When did you say that happened?"

2. Clarifying questions. Often a child or young person is confused about his problems and he con-

veys this confusion to you as he talks. The clarifying question is important as it may help the camper to become more aware of his own thoughts. It assists him to present them in a less confused and more logical manner. Example: "Why do you think he didn't like you then?" "How do you think that happened?" "Can you suggest a reason why they did that?"

3. Reflective questions. This is the type of a question which reflects back to the camper a portion of what he has said. This is helpful as it enables a person to decide whether what he has just said is really what he means. Example: Camper: "You know, the way the others in this cabin treat me, it's as though I don't even exist. They treat me like dirt sometimes. I wish I'd never come to this camp. I wanted to once, but when you are in a cabin where everyone else hates you, it's no fun." Counselor: "They all hate you?"

4. Confronting questions. This is the type of question that is used sparingly when others haven't been very effective. This question is a much more directive type and it may be used when a camper is unable to recognize what his behavior is doing to him. This actually helps a person to examine the meaning of his actions. Camper: "Well, I guess I showed that wise guy from cabin 4. We haven't been getting along all week and he's been bullying me, but when he ran into that tree during the game, did I ever laugh and rub it in!" Counselor: "You laughed at him. Why was that?" Camper: "Well, it was kind of funny and I wanted to get back at him." Counselor: "How do you think he felt when

you laughed at him? Do you think this might keep him from bullying you more this week?"

These are just a sampling of some of the questions which you can use to help your campers. Just as you listen and ask questions, you can also make comments and statements concerning what has been said.

1. Reflective comments. Often a camper attempts to sort out his thoughts and feelings, but has difficulty doing so. This is the opportunity for you to assist by restating what he has said, but in somewhat different terminology. For the most part emphasize the intellectual content of what has been said and clarify it. It is most effective in helping the camper clarify the problem.

Example: Camper: "The other day, I was surprised when the others in my dorm came up and offered to help me. It really shocked me and I wondered why they did it. They didn't have to, and I didn't ask them to. No one else has ever done this. I really wondered why, but after awhile, I started thinking that maybe they're trying to put into practice what the speaker has been talking about and then I wondered if I would have done that." Counselor: "They're helping you surprised you, but perhaps they're putting the teaching into practice and you're not sure if you would do the same or not."

2. Empathetic comments. Empathy is very different from sympathy. Sympathy is not always helpful whereas empathy is indispensable for any type of counseling. Sympathy is mostly emotional and often an identification with the person. Empathy is more

of an intellectual process in which the counselor attempts to put himself momentarily in the camper's situation without emotional involvement. The word means literally "feeling into," whereas sympathy is "feeling with." Empathy has a much deeper sense of involvement or identification with the other person. It's the thinking or feeling of one person into another so that some state of identification is achieved. You attempt in a sense to be with or inside the other person and experience the situation from his point of view and perspective. Example: Camper: "He really hurt me when he broke up with me after the meeting tonight (crying). He said he didn't care about me any more and didn't want to date me and now he's thinking of going out with my best girl friend." Counselor: "This is pretty hard on you right now." Camper: (Nodding head in agreement) "It's about the worst thing that's ever happened to me. It's too much." Counselor: "It's almost more than you can handle right now."

3. Puzzling comments. Some campers react in a negative manner when you are direct with them. This type of comment is usually well accepted and can frequently be of great value. When you appear puzzled by what he has said either through your facial expression, attitude or statement, this causes him to re-express himself or clarify what he has said. In turn, this motivates him to rethink or evaluate what he expressed. Phrases on your part can be unfinished, such as "you mean that . . ." or "if I understand you correctly . . ." or "I think I missed what you meant by that."

4. Confronting comments. This comment is one

that is intended to bring the camper face to face with some phase of his behavior or problem that he hasn't recognized or admitted. This is the type of technique that should be used after some of the less threatening ones have been employed. A camper who is defensive about his behavior and fails to see how he contributes to the problem may have to be confronted directly. Camper: "Boy, I don't know what to do now. The camp dean really let me have it last night. He said my attitude was det . . . oh, what was that word . . . yeah, detrimental to the whole camp. That's what the guy said. He even had the nerve to say that I griped too much about everything and everybody, and all I wanted to be was a critic. Garbage! I think the dean's all wet! So I do say what I think and some of the things here are pretty crumby. He doesn't have to talk to me like that! I've got my opinion, just like anyone else. He treats me like I was an immature kid, instead of a high school senior. After all, I'll be a college man next year." Counselor: "Do you think that perhaps he feels you act like an immature kid and this is why you deserve to be treated like one?"

5. Continuation comment. This is a comment that enables the camper to continue talking. Perhaps he has become frustrated and bogged down and his mind has gone blank. He can't quite succeed in putting his feelings into words and here you help by making a remark that helps him to continue talking. This increases rapport between the two and indicates that you understand what he says and what he means. Example: Camper: "I don't know what's the matter with me. I try so hard to live like

a Christian and then blooey—I wreck it all. Just when I think I'm living straight, then I go and blow it. I know what's right and wrong, but I—I just can't seem to keep with it—and—well—I don't know—I—" Counselor: "You know what's right and yet you have a difficult time doing it and you can't figure it out." Camper: "Yeah, that's just about it. I want to do what's right and I know what to do, but then I goof it all up and fall right back into the old pattern. You know? Like the other day I started . . ."

Other times you may have to structure a situation. A camper comes to you and has the desire to talk but doesn't know how to begin or what to expect from you. You may have to suggest to him that he can just talk about anything on his mind or that is troubling him. You try to work with him to understand his problem and help him to come to a solution.

Another method is to use an understatement of the problem. A camper is more apt to respond to an understatement than an overstatement.

On other occasions, you may have to redirect the responsibility for an answer back to the camper if you feel that he can make the decision or answer the question himself. He may ask you to answer questions, or tell him what to do or say. A response such as, "Well, how do you feel about that" or "what do you think should be done here," will thrust the responsibility back to its proper place.

Another time, you may have to convey the feeling that you accept what is being said. This doesn't mean you agree or disagree with what's being expressed but you do understand or are attempting to understand. Example: "Yes." "Hhmm." "I see."

Now and then, you can provide openings or opportunity for discussion by simply saying, "Well, how are things going with you today?" or "You seem to be a little down in the dumps today. What's up?"

Three other types of remarks that you can make are interpretation, approval and reassurance. Interpretations are when you point out casual relationships or respond to feelings or ideas that have not as yet been expressed by the camper.

Approval statements are the kind where you evaluate the camper or his ideas in such a way that you provide emotional support.

Reassurance is actually encouraging the person, by raising his self-esteem or self-assurance.

In the more directive approach to counseling, you take the responsibility for discovering the nature of the problem and the solution. This method should be reserved for those occasions when the camper is unable to discover the basis of his problem and lacks the necessary insight for a solution. There are occasions when your years of maturity, experience and insight can be of value as you offer suggestions and point out relationships and alternatives. Most novice counselors have the tendency to say "You should do this," or "this is your problem," or "you should never do it that way." The camper may begin to tune out your advice. Being directive doesn't allow him to fully express himself nor establish a two-way communication with you. A sparing use of this technique may prove to be the answer with some campers.

These are the counseling techniques—use them wisely and well. Become acquainted with them before you counsel. Remember, your job is to listen, reflect and clarify. It is not to solve a camper's problems, but to help and assist him to gain insight so that he may find the solution to his problem. When insight is developed, you may be able to present Scripture that will deal with the problem involved. Avoid being preachy in doing this and let the Scriptures speak to your camper. Caution yourself not to give a personal passage of Scripture or pray with him before he has gained insight about the problem. Prayerfully consider when your camper is ready and receptive for your witness.

Consider these recommendations as you counsel:

1. Counseling, to be beneficial, requires a great deal of time. Changes in personality come slowly. Casual advice cannot be construed as counseling.

2. If you do not have highly technical training avoid dealing with difficult cases; rather, they should refer them to an expert in this line. Unskilled counseling may do more harm than good. Recognize the limitations of the layman. Do not use the term "psychoanalyze," and do not attempt psychoanalytic technique.

3. Keep confidences inviolate. If you betray a trust you lose forever your opportunity to be of further help.

4. The best attitude for you to take is that of cheerful, thoughtful objectivity; avoid pronounced sympathizing or condemning. At the same time, of course, show sincere interest and understanding. Learn to be a good listener.

5. Your suggestions may be temporarily useful, but the real solution to a problem can only be discovered by the camper. Instead of trying to impose your will, attempt to help the camper reach his own conclusions and express them in action.

6. The problem as presented may seem to the person in trouble to be insoluble. Even if this were true, he would have to adjust himself to the situation and, therefore, needs help. His problem, however, is probably not unique. Try to see another person in each predicament, and consider how he might solve it.

7. Strange as it may seem, even one who comes voluntarily for help frequently resists your effort to aid him. This resistance may take the form of tardiness, of absence from appointment, of talk about irrelevant matters, and of counter-attacks against you or others. This attitude is not necessarily cause for discouragement.

8. Help the camper to discover and understand all of the facts bearing on the case. He may have difficulty in understanding his problem because he does not know or understand all of the facts. At times these facts will be technical and will need interpretation by an expert.

9. Avoid trying to explain his behavior. By use of other cases and by questioning, build up in his mind his own reasonable interpretation. The aim of the talk is to get him to understand his actions.

10. Expect patterns. Great similarity will be found as far as the behavior of individuals is concerned. For instance, many people fear meeting new situations, wish to avoid people, want to run away from

a situation, try to project the blame onto someone else, make a mountain out of a molehill.

11. Avoid being maneuvered into emotional behavior. Campers will endeavor to arouse sympathy, to shock you, to hurt you with cutting phrases, to inflate your vanity, to get caresses, to make you pity and care for them, to win rebuke, to provoke outbursts of your own ideas, and so forth. Objectivity takes constant defense.

12. Consider physical condition. Many problems are rooted in bad health. This calls for reliable examination and treatment.

13. Begin at the point where the camper finds difficulty. It may not be the root of the problem, but it is the place where he needs help. It will probably lead to the major problem.

14. So far as possible, where mutual adjustment with other people is involved, work out a solution in the presence of all persons concerned. It is sometimes more necessary to study people who live with the individual than the individual himself.

15. In helping a person to solve his problem, it is seldom possible to depend exclusively upon either bringing about changes in environment or upon the camper securing new insight and attitudes. Both are usually in need of some readjustment.

16. Do not let the channels of exploration be determined by emotional reaction. It is sometimes necessary to say things which hurt the camper. If you are sure the surgery is needed, go ahead calmly.

17. Avoid dependence upon verbal solutions. Test them in action.

18. Don't try to save your own face. In many

respects, you may be less well-adjusted than the camper. Grow with him; don't reach down a helping hand from too high up.

19. One easy and frequently helpful step is to remove the camper's fear that he is the only person in the world with his type of difficulty.

20. Avoid focussing on too distant goals without adequate attention to immediate steps. Help the camper to plan steps for improvement now.

21. Even when the simplest words and illustrations have been used, be sure that you will be understood, especially if you are talking about a camper's weaknesses.

22. Watch for budding stereotypes. Don't try to classify a certain person or type of behavior without investigation. Intuition may mislead you often if it is not discounted.

23. Occasionally, overhaul your motives in counseling. Give due weight to the vicarious thrill of hearing about misdeeds, the sense of mastery, the delight in secret intimacy, the desire for affection and trust from the young, the enjoyment of a reputation. Try to keep these in proper proportion to the desire for the welfare of the camper.

24. Encourage independence. If the camper continuously depends on you for help, you are unsuccessful. Give only as much help as is absolutely required and reduce this amount constantly. The person who can get along without you is better off than one whom you constantly help.*

*Ott, Elmer. *So You Want to Be a Camp Counselor.* New York, Association Press, 1946, Pages 29-32.

A camper may seek you out following the Bible study, evening meeting, free time or cabin devotions. Leading a person to Jesus Christ can take place at any time at a camp. Cabin devotions in the evening can be a very rewarding experience. You're alone with just your campers and each one has the opportunity to talk now. You want to know what he is thinking. This is the time to ask and provoke questions. You can lead into this by re-emphasizing or rephrasing what the speaker presented that day or by asking questions about what was stated. "What do you like about camp?" and "what have you learned so far?" Later during the camp, questions such as "what do you think a Christian is?" and "what is a Christian like?" will give you an understanding of his comprehension and readiness to make a commitment. The prayer time in the cabin can be a wonderful experience and can awaken the need within a person for Jesus Christ.

Your goal in counseling with a person about Christ is not just a "decision" but a changed life. Christ assumes the center point in his life. Camps that emphasize the number of "decisions" as such, sometimes face the problem of creating too much pressure on the campers for decisions and end up with some that are superficial. The Holy Spirit must lead in the life of every person to convict him and awaken his need. No commitment should be forced. This is a matter of guidance, not pressure.

The lasting results of a decision made when the individual is mentally and emotionally disturbed are questionable. This was pressed home in a striking and tragic case one time. During a college-age conference one winter, a young man was in attendance who had a multitude of personal problems. He was very impressed with the camp and during the evening communion service appeared very bothered and concerned. After the meeting most of the campers were walking outside in the snow. Suddenly this young man came rushing into the building screaming and crying. He wanted desperately to talk with someone about his problems. A counselor talked with him for over an hour and attempted to assist and counsel him but he remained highly disturbed. Later that evening, he talked with one of the speakers until the wee hours in the morning. He gave all indications of having accepted Jesus Christ as his personal Saviour.

The next evening during a testimony time at his church he gave an extremely dramatic and flowery account of his experience and what he was now going to accomplish. Three weeks later, he was back living the type of life that he had been accustomed to and in the coming year, despite efforts to help him, continued in this path. With this boy, the Holy Spirit had not been the motivating factor.

When you are leading a person to Christ, enough time must be taken to be sure that the individual is not too distraught to understand what he is doing. How much you will have to explain about salvation will largely depend upon his previous experience and background. Each one is different and you will have to determine his knowledge and understanding of the Scriptures. Know what he is seeking. The speaker will present the message, will challenge him and give him the opportunity to express his desire for commitment to Christ. Your task is to instruct the camper in his decision for Christ. The Scriptures must be used and reference made to them as you work with the person concerning his decision. Make sure that he understands what he is doing and show him that his belief and assurance is founded upon the Scripture.

The more extensive your knowledge and comprehension of the Bible is, the better qualified you will be in using the Scripture. Many basic passages should be known from memory so that you have them at your fingertips. Don't confuse the camper with too many Scriptures. As you work with the person, always use the Bible, even if you know the passage from memory. Use the open Bible and, if possible, have him read the passage aloud. Then you can ask him if he understands what he has read.

There are certain basic facts that should be covered from the Scriptures.

1. The need. Romans 3:10,23; 6:23.
2. God's provision for the need. I Peter 2:24; Isaiah 53:5,6; Romans 5:8.
3. He must do something about the provision of God. Ephesians 2:8,9; Revelation 3:20; John 1:12.

Another way of presenting the Scripture is this:

1. The fact of sin. Romans 3:23.
2. The penalty of sin. Romans 6:23.

3. The penalty must be paid. Hebrews 9:27.
4. The penalty was paid by Christ. Romans 5:8.
5. Salvation is a free gift. Ephesians 2:8,9.
6. He must accept this. John 1:12.

From a biblical point of view the camper should be shown how he invites Christ into his life.
1. It is a matter of personally inviting Jesus Christ into his life. Revelation 3:20; Romans 10:10.
2. Jesus Christ has promised that he will come into a person's life if he asks believing. John 6:37.

After the Scriptures have been thoroughly read and explained, have the person pray out loud first and then you pray. Don't pray in place of the camper as this is his time of decision and dedication. You may have to explain to him how to pray and what he can say in his prayer. As you explain prayer to the camper, mention that it is talking to God just as he talks to his friends. God is not interested in big words or solemn tones, but simply wants to hear what is upon his heart. Many will be praying for the first time and the words may come in a hesitant, simple and brief manner. When you follow with your prayer, use simple words and thoughts and don't try to impress the camper with your grasp of theological terms and polysyllabic words.

The camper's prayer should include a recognition that he is a sinner and has done wrong in the sight of God. A realization that Christ died for his sins and then an invitation for Christ to come into his life and become Lord and Master. Remember that the prayers and the expressions will vary. If a proper time of explanation and discussion takes place before the prayer, you will be assured that there is understanding, even if his prayer doesn't completely cover everything you've talked about. If the camper's prayer seems inadequate or if it is too brief for you, don't ask him to pray again and cover the areas that he neglected. Prayer is a spontaneous matter and each of us has had to learn how to pray. The fact that he has now prayed and discovered this access to God will be a thrilling experience and one that he will want to repeat daily.

Well, you say, so that's what is involved and what they mean by counseling. Not exactly, your work has just begun. You've been given the privilege of securing the commitment of the camper. Many others were just as involved in this act as you were. Others were praying for this person. The speaker, and perhaps the pastor back home laid the groundwork for this decision.

If you ever lead a person to Christ and stop there, you've failed in your counseling ministry. What is called follow-up or Christian growth must begin immediately and continue during the remainder of the conference. It must continue, even when the camper returns to his church. It is tremendously important that you lay a solid foundation on which to build his spiritual life. There is never enough time to work in this realm. In a sense, you will be raising him until he is able to care for himself and in turn go out and spiritually help someone else. If you fail in this task, who will be the one to do it? You are the one in a position to follow through. Perhaps one of the speakers had the privilege of leading your camper to Christ. You will still be the person involved with his follow-up process.

There are many different methods to use in the follow-up program. Because each camper is a distinct personality, it is best to try to fit the material to his need and this necessitates some flexibility. There are some specifics to cover: You have been born into the family of God. The Holy Scriptures speak of it as being "born again," John 3:1-13. Before this time, you had nothing in common with God because you were a sinner. But now a relationship has been established with God by your acceptance of Jesus Christ. In a sense, you are a baby in the relationship with God. As a child, you need to grow. The growth process takes place as you feed on spiritual food and this food is in the Bible, I Peter 2:2,3; Hebrews 5:13,14. You receive this spiritual food by reading the Bible, II Timothy 2:15; Jeremiah 15:16. This should be a daily occurrence. The Bible becomes a part of you as you read it, study it and memorize it, Deuteronomy 11:18; Joshua 1:8; Psalm 119:11.

Many camps and churches are using the B-rations produced by the Navigators. This is the first of several memory booklets that have been devised and constructed for the new Christian. This includes the assurance of salvation, I John 5:11,12. The Christian life is a definite fact and not just an emotional experience. If you have received him, he is yours.

Camps vary in their method of recording decisions, but some records should be kept. They are an aid to help camps and counselors in their follow-up program and the interest evidenced can be very meaningful for the camper. Some use a record form or decision card where the person writes out the decision that he has made on two portions of the card. One portion is kept for the camp records and is then sent on to this person's church. The camper himself keeps the other portion.

Another method which has personal meaning for the author is that of the letter. When I met Jesus Christ face to face at a summer conference in high school, I was asked to put in writing the decision that I made and why and what this meant to me. The letter was dated and placed in a self-addressed envelope. The camp kept this and six months later, I received a letter in the mail addressed to me in my own handwriting. Was I ever surprised to see the letter that I had written that previous summer, and it did have an impact! It was a reminder of a commitment that I personally had made and it made me think, what am I doing about it now? Several years later as I was preparing for the ministry, I was sorting through some boxes and folders of materials that I had been keeping for years, and once again, ran into this same letter. How precious it was to read in simple words (and poor handwriting) the decision that changed the course of my life! I still have that letter.

While at that same camp, I had an opportunity during the closing night fagot service to write my testimony in the camp testimony book. I can remember going before several hundred young people and giving my testimony and then writing in this book. I've gone back to that book several times during the past years and what a meaningful experience that night was and continues to be. I have the assurance of the new birth and can point to the time in my life when it took place.

The assurance of victory, I Corinthians 10:13. Temptation is real and troublesome. The continual questions of new and mature Christians concerning temptation are evident. When a person accepts Christ, the Lord actually comes into his life in the person of the Holy Spirit. His body is the temple of the living God (I Corinthians 3:16). The Holy Spirit makes him conscious of things in his life that are contrary to what God wants. There will be temptations but God knows the capacity of his endurance and will give him the strength to overcome the temptation.

The assurance of forgiveness, I John 1:9. God tells us to confess our sins and then we have the assurance of forgiveness, no matter what the sin may have been. God wants us to realize that we have done wrong and that there is a remedy for the transgression.

The assurance of provision, John 16:24. A person's joy can be full when he prays in Christ's name. As you talk with the person, you should underscore the fact that the Christian life is not easy. It takes everything that he can give, it is a life of discipline, drive and sacrifice. The Christian life is a life of faith (Colossians 2:6,7). A walk is merely a succession of steps and one step is taken at a time. The Christian life is the same and each step is a commitment to Jesus Christ (Galatians 5:16,25). This life is lived by believing, just as the new birth comes by believing. A person runs into difficulty trying to live the Christian life but finds it is possible if he trusts Christ to live through him. This life is a life of dependence upon Christ (Psalm 62:5; Proverbs 3:5,6).

Encourage and attempt to create an opportunity for the new Christian to tell someone else about his decision while he is at camp. Let him tell another camper who is a Christian, a non-Christian, one of the speakers or have him share a testimony before the entire group (Romans 10:9,10). Sharing before the entire camp is one of the easier places to testify. In the audience are many who have had the same experience and they are sympathetic and understand what the camper is expressing.

There must be some practical encouragement and guidance to help him face the problems that he will meet back home. Unless distance prevents, attempt to have personal contacts with him as often as possible. If his home is too remote, write often. Notify his home church of his decision so that it can assist him in his Christian growth. Present Bible study helps and methods to him while at camp. Work with him and establish a Bible study pattern before the conference has been completed. This will take persistence on your part. In each remaining day of camp, take time and meet with him. Encourage and show him how to study his Bible. He may sense the need, but lack the method. Let him progress at his own pace and not yours.

Show him the value and method of memorizing Scripture. Assign for memory as many verses as he thinks he can learn before camp concludes. Let him know you will check on these verses each day. In addition to systematic Bible study, teach him how to pray. Pray with him and show him the importance of a regular quiet time with God. Help him make and use a prayer list.

Be careful not to exclude the older Christian from your personal attention. He, too, will profit from this individual counsel and concern. Successful counselors meet individually with each of their campers at least once during a camp. A suggestion list of helps and booklets may be beneficial:

"Born to Reproduce" by Dawson Trotman. Published by the Back to the Bible Broadcast.

"My Heart, Christ's Home" by Robert Munger. Inter-Varsity Press.

"Quiet Time." Published by Inter-Varsity.

"Teach Yourself the Bible Series" by Keith L. Brooks. Correspondence School, Moody Bible Institute.

"Studies in Christian Living." Bible study and Scripture memorization program. Published by The Navigators, Colorado Springs, Colorado.

"Ten Basic Steps Toward Christian Maturity." Campus Crusade.

"The Basics." Published by Youth for Christ International.

"Search The Scriptures" method of Bible Study. Billy Graham Evangelistic Association.

"What the Bible Is All About" by Henrietta Mears. Regal Books, Gospel Light Publications.

"Growth by Groups." Christian Outreach. Huntingdon Valley, Penn. 19006.

These are just a few of the many published

materials available. Most of these are for older teens and above, but there are several available for younger campers. Individual churches, denominations and conference grounds will have suggestions and many of their own materials. No matter what you use, be certain to establish some type of regular Bible study program with your campers. Helps such as these will be very useful.

TOPICAL SCRIPTURE REFERENCES

A. Sin

What is it?

I John 3:4	Transgression of the law
I John 5:17	All unrighteousness
James 4:17	To know to do good and doeth it not
John 16:9	Unbelief

Who are sinners?

Romans 3:23	All have sinned
Isaiah 53:6	All we like sheep
Romans 3:10	None righteous

Result of sin

Romans 5:12	Death passed to all men
Romans 6:23	Wages of sin is death
John 8:24	Ye shall die in your sins

God's Solution

John 3:16	Shall not perish, have everlasting life

I John 5:12	He that hath the Son hath life
Romans 5:8	While yet sinners, Christ died for us
I John 1:9	Confess sins, he will forgive

B. Born Again (new birth)

John 3:3	Must be born again
II Corinthians 5:17	In Christ a new creature
John 1:12	Power to become the sons of God
Galatians 2:20	New life in Christ
I Peter 1:23	Born by the Word of God
John 3:6	New birth necessary

C. Salvation

Ephesians 2:8,9	Saved by grace through faith
John 5:24	Everlasting life by hearing and believing
Romans 5:1	Justified by faith we have peace
Acts 13:39	All that believe are justified

D. Assurance

II Timothy 1:12	He is able to keep
I Peter 1:5	Kept by the power of God
Philippians 1:6	Confidence of God finishing what he started
Ephesians 2:10	We are created unto good works

John 1:12	As many as received him are sons
Romans 8:38,39	Nothing can separate us from him

E. Dedication

Psalm 37:5	Commit thy way unto the Lord
Proverbs 3:5,6	Trust in the Lord, acknowledge him, he shall direct thy paths

F. Prayer

Proverbs 15:8	The prayer of the upright is his delight . . . pray for one another
James 5:16	The effectual prayer of a righteous man
I Thessalonians 5:17	Pray without ceasing

G. The Bible

Isaiah 40:8	The word of our God shall stand forever
Ephesians 6:17	and the sword of the Spirit which is the word of God
Hebrews 4:12	The word of God is quick
I John 2:14	The word of God abides in you

H. God

Isaiah 12:2	Behold God is my salvation

Isaiah 40:28	The Lord is the everlasting God
Philippians 2:13	For God is at work in you

I. Growing Spiritually

Ephesians 3:17-19	that Christ may dwell in your hearts
Colossians 1:9-11	we . . . do not cease to pray for you
Colossians 3:16	Let the word of God dwell in you richly, in all wisdom
II Timothy 2:15	Study to shew thyself approved unto God
I Peter 2:2	Like newborn babes, desire the sincere milk of the word
II Peter 1:5-8	Supplement your faith with virtue
II Peter 3:18	Grow in the grace and knowledge of our Lord and Saviour

J. Temptation

Isaiah 41:10	Fear thou not, for I am with thee
I Corinthians 10:13	There hath no temptation taken you
Philippians 1:6	He that hath begun a good work in you will perform it
II Thessalonians 3:3	But the Lord is faithful, who shall stablish you

This is counseling. Overwhelming you say! To some, it can appear that way, and yet when you consider that God is faithful and gives you stability, courage and the ability to realize your potential, the task becomes less frightening. Claim II Corinthians 4:16 as your verse for comfort and reassurance as a camp counselor. "Therefore we do not become discouraged—utterly spiritless, exhausted, and wearied out through fear, though our outer man is (progressively) decaying and wasting away, yet our inner self is being (progressively) renewed day after day" (Amplified Bible). Two verses in Jeremiah promise you great possibilities. "Behold, I am the Lord, the God of all flesh; is there anything too hard for me?" "Call unto me, and I will answer thee, and show thee great and mighty things, which thou knowest not" Jeremiah 32:27; 33:3.

COUNSELOR - COUNSELING EVALUATION AND TRAINING SHEET	Yes	No	Partly-unsure	Comments
Did you talk more than the counselee?				
What percent of the conversation was dominated by you?				
Was this person able to express what he wanted to express?				
Did you keep your mind on what he was saying or did it wander?				
Were you able to understand what he said?				

	Yes	No	Partly-unsure	Comments
Do you feel that you were directive with him?				
Do you think he felt rejected by you?				
Did you feel like "punishing" him?				
Did you try to "impress" or "shock" him?				
Did you attempt to clarify the problem for him?				
If you used Scripture, did you know what Scripture to use and where to find it?				
Was the Scripture used in proper context?				
Did you have him read the Scripture?				
If prayer was a part of this time, did he pray?				
Would he want to come back and talk with you again?				
Was he able to interrupt you?				
Did he feel that he could disagree with what you said?				
Did you try to influence him as to what he should talk about?				
Were you a good listener?				
Do you feel that anything was accomplished?				

	Yes	No	Partly-unsure	Comments
Did you push for the type of decision that you thought he should make?				
Did you seek a decision too soon?				
Did you think about things that had no connection with his problem?				
Did he feel free to say anything he wanted without fear of censure from you?				
Did you have a negative reaction to what he expressed?				
Did you feel anger or hostility toward him?				
If you did, can you determine why?				
Do you know the difference between empathy and sympathy?				
Was there a feeling of empathy present?				
Did he initiate the discussion?				
Did he take an active role in it?				
If any conclusions were drawn, did he make them and have a choice in doing so?				
Do you think that he felt he was being understood?				
Did you question him during the conversation?				
Did you use a variety of questions?				

So...What Do I Do Now?

Chapter 7

John is a new camper this year. He has never been away from home before and he is giving his counselor fits! He is constantly in trouble. If he can't have his own way or has a dispute with another camper, he simply lashes out in a fit of anger and hits the other person. He seems very tense and can't talk out these disagreements. When he is approached about his difficulties with others, he feels there wasn't anything wrong with settling disputes his way. Why would a young person act like this?

Investigation reveals that the source of John's

problem goes back to his home environment. His parents are constantly fighting and arguing. There hasn't been love in this home for some time. From time to time the parents separate, but then come back together again and try to get along. This is done more for economic reasons than for any other motivation. They are very hostile toward one another and fight every day with the result being physical violence.

This is the type of home that John lives in and the atmosphere is one of stress and tension. He has little opportunity at home to see people solve problems aside from the use of force and physical pressure. John is a tense boy because he lives in a tense home. He fights and uses physical force because this is all he knows and it is merely a way of solving a problem. Perhaps this is acceptable behavior at home, but it isn't at camp. Before you judge why a person misbehaves at camp, know the motivation behind the action.

You as a counselor are in a position to influence the campers during an important time in their lives. The problems that you face are those of having people from diverse homes and varied backgrounds. You will have to adjust to each one and enable them to adjust to one another and the camp program. Habits which have been entrenched over the years will be hard to break, but you still have a responsibility to help the individuals. Some will need to change their behavior patterns and attitudes and will attempt to do so, but won't make very much progress. You'll have to learn how to reach each camper and influence his conduct. You will also need an understanding of the "why" of his behavior.

Why do campers misbehave? This is a question that all counselors ask at one time or another. There are a number of suggested reasons that can be presented. Remember that some campers may have these motivations for their behavior and many may not. Each one may have a different drive that causes him to behave in the manner that he does. You want to know the reason for the act. You are interested in the "why" something was done.

Some guidance clinics have stated that most behavior cases can be classified into three categories:

1. The excessively inhibited person. This is the person who is very tense and inwardly nervous, but outwardly conforms. Why? Because this is the only way he feels that he can gain approval. Often this is because his parents are cold, critical individuals and their favor has to be won. Generally, he presents few or no problems, but often he is worse off than the one who lashes out and is overt in his misbehavior.

2. The excessively uninhibited person. Basically, this one is unsocialized and you know when he is present! Many are aggressive and have great difficulty achieving good interpersonal relations. They are in constant conflict with others. The behavior that you see is a symptom of their problems.

3. The well-adjusted person. The other type of behavior pattern is that of the person who is an acceptable and loyal member of his own group. Basically, he maintains good interpersonal relations.

Rudolf Dreikurs presents a different theory in his

book, "Children: The Challenge." He discusses the view that many children pursue "mistaken goals." The first of these is the desire for undue attention. Many discouraged children use this to help them feel that they belong. The second mistaken goal is the struggle for power. This comes about because of a clash or conflict between a child and adult. The child disobeys to exert his power and won't conform to a higher power. When the power contest is intensified, then some children choose the third goal, which is retaliation and revenge. The fourth "mistaken goal" is generally chosen by a discouraged child. He attempts to demonstrate his complete inadequacy. He gives up entirely and takes a helpless attitude. This helplessness enables him to avoid unpleasant tasks. For a complete and thorough discussion of these "goals" and methods of working with them, it is recommended that the above mentioned book be consulted.

There are divergent theories concerning the why of behavior. The most accepted and recognized will be discussed here. Every person has basic or emotional needs and requirements. These must be given and presented even to the smallest child and on throughout his life.

What are these basic needs? First of all, there must be affection and acceptance. When this is present, there is a sense of inner contentment, or of well being. Acceptance involves feeling wanted by others and belonging to a home and family, and even to a dorm at a weekend camp. We need to be able to share our thoughts and feelings with others, to let our hair down and be totally and completely honest, and to experience others liking us when we are this way. The feeling of love must be conveyed; this is the basic need.

People also have a need for power. This is the desire to show or feel power over something or someone. This drive can be directed and the need fulfilled when a camper derives satisfaction in the making of a pair of moccasins in the craft hut, completing a ten-mile hike, or mastering the jack-knife dive at the pool. This can also be achieved by performing one's job well on a camp council. Misdirected or displaced power creates the bully, the disobedient and stubborn camper or one who exhibits temper tantrums. This can also be evidenced in lying, dawdling and procrastinating.

The drive for security is another basic need that we all experience. Many campers will miss the security derived at home when they first come to camp and the reactions to this will be varied.

There is also the drive for recognition and achievement. The person needs to develop the conviction that he can accomplish something and that he is adequate enough to meet life head-on. At the same time, he needs others to see and recognize that he can accomplish something in this life.

These wishes or drives are present in all of your campers as they are present in all normal people. They do, however, vary in intensity. Recognizing that these are fundamental drives may help you understand and interpret more correctly camper behavior. The well-adjusted person seeks to satisfy these in socially acceptable ways, but when the person becomes frustrated or feels that he isn't satisfying them, he often resorts to unapproved devices.

Certain campers will attempt to fulfill these needs at the expense of others. We need to listen, hear, and watch so that we can sense and understand what our campers are feeling. Many times, misbehavior means that the camper has some unsatisfied emotional needs or that he is expressing hurt, anger or fear because the needs weren't met in his past. We try as much as possible in a limited amount of time, to help satisfy those needs.

Other problems can come about because of the counselor himself. The relationship between you and the camper is crucial. See that the campers are satisfied and adjusting to the program. Your attempt to force adult values or adherence to plans and procedures will initiate unrest and agitation. Resentment against over-severe, or worse than that, inconsistent discipline in camp will have its results.

Boredom, idleness, or too much energy with too little to do will be evidenced by mischievous behavior. Boredom must not be thought of just in terms of not having anything to do and a lack of interesting activities. This is basic to becoming bored, but other factors influence the camper.

Forcing him to participate in an activity that isn't to his liking; frustration because of inadequate and unadaptable equipment, and a military type of exacting schedule will create a bored and disinterested camper.

A problem on the other extreme is the over-demanding program which drains the camper of his energy, and then you have one who falls asleep during the meetings or fireside devotional time, making him overly sensitive and crabby. The lack of proper rest following the meals, or poor quality food can contribute to the deteriorated physical condition of a camper.

The camp or conference grounds may unwittingly be the cause of disorder. Poor facilities, uncomfortable seats, hot stuffy rooms, a meeting outdoors when the temperature is too cold or windy, poor lighting, not enough room, and distractive noises or disturbances will hamper the progress of the camp. These, however, will usually create just minor disturbances such as restlessness, talking, inattention and drowsiness.

Other campers may experience fear, rejection, or feeling alone in an overwhelming crowd. Fear may be caused by the lack of familiar surroundings, or by being away from the security of home, church and friends. Be sensitive to the feelings of a camper, as we never know what remark by others will give him the feeling of being rejected.

Another may feel like a displaced person because of the numbers at camp or in his dorm, and he isn't used to this type of close living. Some may feel rejected because of a basic feeling and attitude of inferiority. This could be centered in an actual handicap and slow development. It could very well be an unfounded fear, but just as real to the camper as one based on fact.

Some of your most pressing problems may come from church or Christian homes. Quite often, these campers react against authority and their faith as they haven't had any opportunity to express their doubts and raise the questions that have been plaguing them for years. Because they were brought up within the church, they have adhered to an expected behavior pattern. They have developed a spiritual facade with no internalization of the Christian values. Others from this group will react as a matter of showing their independence and resentment against the church or parents.

The following is a list of some of the camp behavior problems that you may encounter. The timid or lonesome camper, the coward, the hypochondriac or one who pretends he is sick, the nervous camper, the bed wetter, the sissy, the seclusive person, daydreamer, liar, overdependent, unresponsive, lethargic, selfish, stubborn, restless, over-active.

Some will have habits of poor eating, sleeping, speech, nail biting, thumb sucking and masturbation. Still others will exhibit traits like: teasing, bullying, fighting, stealing, showing off, temper tantrums, disobedience, destructiveness, swearing, sexual problems, overcritical, faultfinding and the "know-it-all." There will also be those who won't follow peer leadership.

This is not the end of the world, nor is it the most pleasant counseling experience you will ever have. When one of these rears its head, you must handle it. Hopefully, the suggestions presented within this book will enable you to work with these problems.

First, meet Milton Milquetoast. He appears to be timid. He avoids contact with others at camp and seems to retreat from everyone and every activity.

Far too often, counselors are pleased to find this quiet, unobtrusive camper, but his can be a very serious problem. His actions may take the form of just withdrawing from camp life and staying to himself. Walking by himself, doing craft alone, daydreaming, hanging back and watching, even disappearing for a time, or staying in the cabin, may be the pattern for Milton. Why would he act this way? What makes him behave like this? Some daydreams offer more satisfaction than the real-life experiences.

He may feel sorry for himself and retreat into his own private world to nurse his wounds and hurts. He may retreat because of a physical deficiency that is too obvious to be comfortable. Perhaps he has been so overprotected in his home environment that his social development has been stifled, even retarded, and he simply doesn't relate well with others in a group. Withdrawing may just be a temporary solution. He can't converse with others in his own peer group. Perhaps this is the first time away from home. He may be dominated at home and thrust into a subjective position. Now he finds it hard to break out of this mold.

In some cases he is less mature or hasn't been to camp before and is overwhelmed with all that he sees taking place. He finds it hard adjusting to everything. It is much safer and easier to retreat than to attempt to break into the busy, eventful life.

Perhaps there is some fear of the opposite sex involved which is of so much concern to him that it hampers his total social development. He may withdraw because of unfavorable experiences in the past, either at school, home, or camp. He doesn't want to take the risk of getting hurt again. Perhaps it was a counselor who did this or perhaps he is afraid of you as his counselor! Now what can you do to help this situation?

1. See if there are any records available at the camp or in the physical report in the nurse's office. Information gained here may shed some light on the "why" of his behavior.

2. Attempt to find the underlying reason for his reaction.

3. Make sure that he is a part of the group and provide him with things to do with other campers who will take an interest in him and accept him just the way he is.

4. Show a sincere interest and concern in him yourself. Remember, this doesn't mean to give sympathy, but be a friend to him.

5. Provide some opportunity for you two to get together and encourage him to talk about himself. This may come about through participating in an activity that will provide him with some enjoyment.

6. Attempt to find a group project or a situation where he can be a part or even learn to take part. Perhaps he has a latent skill that needs developing. This can be a source of pride and satisfaction for him, and the encouragement and recognition that he derives from others will build his confidence. When he feels that he can make a contribution, he will start to construct his sense of confidence. When you do give him something to do, make sure that at first you know that it is something at which he can succeed.

7. In sports or athletic competition, place emphasis on the sportsmanship rather than on winning. Avoid methods of selecting teams that will embarrass him because he isn't picked or he is the last one that is taken and reluctantly at that! Try to assign groups and teams equally. When recognition is given to campers, it can be given to those who have achieved just a little as well as to those who are accustomed to winning because of their physical prowess.

8. Your discussion time with the campers can be used in such a way that he learns to sense and cope with problems. The final stage is to develop an understanding of the reasons for his action and then develop ways of helping one another in a spirit of Christian love.

9. If he withdraws because of unfounded fear, a discussion letting him air his feelings may lead to a better and more logical, realistic understanding and acceptance of the situation.

Closely associated with the first type of problem is Sally Solo. The feeling of loneliness is a pathetic feeling and one of lostness and futility in its severest forms. It can be quite natural for the shy or timid person to be lonely. The causes for this will again vary, but homesickness can contribute to it. The inability to find things of interest in camp, lack of close friends and missing those back home, fear of new friends and of the "rough" camping situation contribute to this feeling of being lonely. Enabling her to "talk it out" may conquer the first hurdle and prepare the road for a different direction on her part. Putting her into group activities in which she is proficient will help to raise her morale and feelings of self-confidence.

The never ending problem of homesickness is something that occurs in most camps, but in varying degrees. It is a longing for the nearness of someone or something that is very close or important to the person. It can be recognized in campers like Harley Homebody. He withdraws or mopes around camp, shows a lack of participation, cries, is sullen. Sometimes he openly states that he is homesick and wants to leave camp this very instant! Perhaps you are surprised that anyone would want to leave the beautiful and refreshing surroundings of any camp to go back to the congestion and hurried pace of life in the cities and suburbs. There are reasons for this feeling and to Harley, it can be a powerful urge and drive.

Quite often, there has been an overattachment between him and his parents. Overindulgence and protection at home doesn't develop self-confidence. They've been afraid to "let go and let grow." This relationship can still be nurtured while he is at camp by incessant calls and letters from his parents. The attachment "back home" may be to special friends and this occurs, not only with the junior age, but with the teens. The involvement with boy and girl friends can dominate his total life perspective at this stage. In some cases, he has been so strongly attached to pets or club programs and activities that the thought of missing these appears to be too much for him!

The camp itself will have some effect upon homesickness. Strange surroundings and the lack of making Harley feel at home or the lack of interest and concern in him will be a detriment. The new atmosphere may contribute to a feeling of insecurity. If he is self-conscious about himself in any way, homesickness is an easy way out of the predicament. For some, this is the first experience in a group situation and the limited privacy or lack of it may be upsetting. Homesickness for some may come when things don't go as they had anticipated. Any lack in the environment that leaves a need unfulfilled may precipitate this feeling.

In many camps and conferences, there are a number of campers who have been sent to camp against their will. Parents either feel that this will be a wonderful educational experience for their child or else it is the most convenient way to have a vacation from their offspring. Shipping them off to camp erases their conscience about wanting them away for a period of time. It has been noted that homesickness doesn't always show itself at the start of a camp but more toward the third and fourth day and particularly around mealtime—and it can be contagious!

What is the basic underlying reason for homesickness? The one term that can sum this up is "fear"! Simple fear is disturbing and, if allowed to grow and develop, can become a very disrupting emotion: fear of being away from familiar surroundings, fear of the unknown—the camp, people and activities.

What can you do as his counselor? If you are counseling for your own church, you may be able to ascertain in advance who your campers will be and arrange to meet them at your church. Call them and get acquainted before the camp begins. The interest that you show at this time will help your relationships later on.

If you are unable to take this approach before the camp, then at the beginning, groundwork must be laid so this problem doesn't develop. Welcome each camper as soon as he arrives. Some camps have welcome signs in the dorm and name tags ready to be pinned on the minute the camper steps into camp. An attractive and homey cabin will add to the desire to stay and make this his home for a time.

The best method is to make each one feel wanted and loved and accepted as a part of the group. You may have to assist him in establishing new friendships. Perhaps you know of one in the cabin who is an old-timer to camping, or perhaps he has the same interest or hobby as this potential homesick fatality. A buddy system may help to get all campers involved quickly.

Be alert for possible signs of this malady. If you have a fellow or girl who tends to go off by himself you may have cause to wonder, especially if this takes place during mealtime or the evening hours.

Physical symptoms or problems like constipation or indigestion or diarrhea are contributing factors. Any type of illness can initiate homesick feelings. The warmth and care that he is used to at home may be missed. If you can get him to stay just one more day or two until that special swim meet is held, he will more than likely remain for the duration of camp. Help him to talk about his feelings.

One of the major ways of combating the first three problems mentioned is to show a special interest in each camper. Yet there may be one who over-responds to this type of treatment and he or she becomes your shadow. Some have referred to Carl Clinger as the "counselor's pet," not because this is your desire and plan but because he has so attached himself to you. He hangs around, even bothers or pesters you. He follows you everywhere and anywhere, even to the bathroom. In many cases, he is trying very hard to please you. He does this because of lack of acceptance by others at camp and in his home. He is trying too hard and you may have to combat your own feelings of impatience, dislike and aversion to him.

This is the pattern that happens with everyone else that shows some interest in him. He tries so hard that people shun him. Because of his forward thrust, he drives people away from him. Ignoring or avoiding his attentions won't work. Perhaps if you get him to work with others, this will help the situation and keep him from hanging around you. Too often, however, this won't solve the problem, for as soon as he has completed his task, he'll be right back.

He may need someone to be very frank with him and tell him what he is doing. Let him know that you like him and accept him and he doesn't have to be around you that much to keep your favor. Indicate to him that he is actually missing out on a good time by not being involved with the others in the cabin. Guide him into some activity. Don't push him onto the others as they probably have some of the initial feelings that you experienced, too.

Daydreaming is natural to most people and has some positive value, but Dawn Dreamer spends her time in reverie and prefers to sit alone and daydream, rather than participate in the interpersonal and sports activities. Excessive daydreaming can be unhealthy. When too much time is devoted to this and the person would rather daydream than establish contacts with children or young people, he has a problem. Your friendship and counsel here may open the door to the reason behind this behavior. Encourage and assist him to break into the group activities.

Most of these problems have dealt with behavior that is marked by withdrawing and seclusiveness. There are situations on the other side of the ledger, too. Campers who present the "wise guy" or "show off" phase are in attendance just as much as the others. Some attempt to dominate all the activities and appoint themselves leader in everything. This occurs even when the others protest and are quite vocal in their reactions toward him.

Some try to overdemonstrate their talents (whether real or imaginary), and a few criticize constantly. Others talk continually and never let anyone else speak his piece. The "know-it-all" attitude is one that is offensive and elicits negative reactions. Lack in patience on your part will make you see this as an action that needs punishment or discipline. In reality this behavior is exhibiting an inner need and lack. You may have seen adults like this, schoolmates, or working associates who fit this description.

Many of the reasons and causes of the withdrawn and timid camper are present here, but the symptoms take a different route. Overindulgence by the parent may have been a factor, or perhaps this is the behavior pattern of his friends or siblings at home, and this is the only way that he knows how to act. In the teen years, physical ability is important, and those who lack it may boast the most. Overcompensation for a weakness may be another reason for having failed in one area, so he is determined to make good in a new one, no matter what.

Once in awhile, you may find what has been termed a "sleeper." This is a person who has leadership potential but it has lain dormant for years or has had no avenue of expression available. Now the person makes an attempt but because of lack of experience and security, he blunders and gropes around. If the camper doesn't receive the attention that he is seeking from this behavior, it loses its impetus and significance. Confront him with his behavior. Explore with him why he thinks that he behaves in this manner. This brings the problem into focus. It may reveal to you many inner feelings and stimulate needed hours of counseling with him.. If there are areas and abilities where he is proficient, provide him with natural and needed outlets where this skill can be exhibited, used, and where the praise received is honest and earned. If he is as good as he thinks he is in some area, then leadership recognition will come to him.

Competence in any area must fit the needs and interest of his fellow campers. Perhaps he has been limited and stifled in his range of interests back home. The home or community could have been lacking in its environmental stimuli and opportunities. Now with the abundance of resources available to you at camp, the possibility of broadening his interest is possible. New recreational activities and athletic events, wildlife, vegetation and foliage, crafts, music—your interest and suggestions may open new horizons heretofore untouched and unthought.

Now and then, one of these campers who is the "know-it-all" will be an instigator of pranks and may even capture the imagination of the others in the dorm and be able to lead and manipulate them but in the wrong direction. Some have been known to threaten the counselors and deliberately and openly flaunt the regulations and the staff. One example may point out how this could be handled.

A young counselor was having difficulty controlling some of the boys in his cabin. They were noisy and didn't want to attend the meetings and had skipped the morning service. Now the boys were all in the cabin talking and laying plans for their next escapade. One older boy, Dave, appeared to be influencing most of the others. The last day or so he had become sarcastic to those in authority. As the counselor stepped into the room, he heard Dave tell the others that there wasn't anything to worry about as no one would catch them and even if they did, nothing would happen to them.

The counselor stepped forward and asked where the boys were during the last meeting and why they hadn't attended. The group fell silent, but

Dave stood his ground and said defiantly, "We didn't feel like coming and we may not attend the one tonight. What are you going to do about it? You can't make us!" The other fellows upon hearing this seemed to find their courage and echoed Dave. They were encouraging him and at the same time delighting in this contest between their cabin mate and counselor. How would you have handled this power struggle?

Fortunately, the counselor, young as he was, had the presence of mind to remove Dave from the group and take him out of earshot of the rest. Had he continued this discussion and discipline in front of the entire cabin of boys, little would have been accomplished. When Dave was alone and didn't have the encouragement and strength from the others, he was a different person and could be talked to in a sensible manner. At the same time, the boys were much more subdued and even mild and obedient without their leader present.

The problem was overcome and better understanding developed between all of the fellows and the counselor. If faced with a similar situation, remove the one antagonist from the group when you talk with him. This is a basic policy in any type of discipline or even reprimanding. Give the person the courtesy of privacy.

Aggressiveness is a very forceful emotion and one that threatens others when they come into contact with it. Again, you may have campers who are overly aggressive. Many counselors experience great feelings of inadequacy when they encounter a camper whose behavior pattern is overly aggressive. Aggression can be caused once again by a lack of security. A lack of love, perhaps, has bred feelings of hostility and anger toward others. In an attempt to reduce tension, he is unable to cope with his frustrations and resorts to aggressive behavior. The effectiveness of this is only temporary and the need is still present. Its forms are many and varied.

You perhaps have encountered this type of individual—the braggart, bully, tough or bossy guy. This individual excels or attempts to, by domineering others, talking too much, taking and using other's belongings, fighting or swearing.

Aggressiveness can take the opposite form, however, and a person can be very aggressive by assuming a passive role. Some have called or labeled this reaction the passive-aggressive role. The person who says that he didn't hear you or delays others or finds ways to irritate people in subtle ways fits this category. Quite often, we fail to recognize some of these reactions as being aggressive. We tend to react more to the outwardly aggressive type. How can you counsel with the person who is aggressive?

A kind, friendly attitude toward him (even when he has dominated others) will break through his veneer and impress upon him that you care about him. He needs someone to care. Help him to establish some friendships and to find some place in the group where he can be accepted. If he can be praised for acceptable behavior and for deeds that are exceptional, this will help. When aggressive campers experience approval for socially acceptable behavior, their need has been fulfilled and they are on the way to learning a better and more effective pattern.

Counselors have been overheard to remark that they have a camper who is never quiet in action or word. He seems to fight constantly and is hyperactive. If you are confronted with a camper like this, take notice. Some fidgetiness is natural, but an excessive amount indicates generally an unhappy person who is troubled and does not know how to meet or deal with the emotional problems that trouble him. These campers are always in motion, squirming, wiggling, fiddling or playing with objects. If finger nails are chewed or bitten, this is one good indication that not all is well within. A child or adolescent who is fidgety likes to keep busy, but often the hyperactive child should have his schedule altered from very strenuous activities to the less active. Slowing the person down, but keeping him occupied, may have a quieting effect upon him.

Another common problem, particularly with the junior age, is that of enuresis or bedwetting. This is something that happens with almost every child at one age or another. With some, it has carried over much later than others. There can be several factors causing this. It could be caused by physical factors or by nervousness or overactivity. It will be to your benefit to check the camper's health record before the first night to see if any have indicated this problem. Other reasons for the problem are lack of early and consistent training in the home, past illness where the person has spent a great deal of time in bed and some because of drinking too much liquid too near bedtime. Most causes, however, tend to be psychological and indicate an inability to satisfy some of his needs.

If you have a camper such as this, you may want to take some basic precautions such as using a rubber sheet on the bed. If bunk beds are used, place this camper on a bottom bunk. Limiting liquids after dinner is necessary and be sure that the person uses the rest room before retiring for the night. Some advocate awakening the person thirty minutes to an hour after retiring and having him go to the rest room again. Don't allow the others to ridicule or haze the camper.

A problem that is difficult to contend with, whether it occurs at camp or at school, is that of stealing. When stealing occurs, people react quickly and perhaps too severely. Most deal solely with the behavioral aspect instead of the motivating factor or cause. The nature of the problem can vary, depending upon the age of the camper and the particular situation. The act can vary from a one-time proposition to a compulsive disorder in which the value of the object is of little importance to the person involved, but the act itself is the significant factor. This type of behavior, if brought out into the open, can result in strained relationships between campers and even physical disagreements.

As is the case with other deviations, the causes are many, but each is important. One reason may be an undeveloped sense of possession. In some cases with campers who come from a materially deprived environment, this may be an acceptable form of behavior. Seeing other campers with possessions that are of greater value and worth, the person sometimes steals in order to join the group of the "haves" instead of the "have-nots."

In some situations, the act of stealing is a cry for help in that he seeks and craves attention, and the need is not being fulfilled. This is one way in which to get others to sit up and take notice of him.

Others resort to stealing because the parents haven't allowed him to have sufficient money of his own to spend as he sees fit. This drives him to obtain, no matter the means.

Some stealing falls into the category of reaction, rebellion against authority, or a way of getting back at either a camper or staff member. When campers have deep rooted psychological problems, the overt behavior can take many forms and stealing may be one of them.

From these causes, it can be stated that you must be careful in dealing with the theft situation as, too often, emotions become aroused when the camper is apprehended or discovered.

In cases involving stealing, it is important to consult with the senior counselor or the boy's or girl's dean, as the case may be. Endeavoring to find out the reason for the behavior must be done in a slow, patient manner with understanding and love. Many campers when confronted may retreat into a shell and be uncommunicative. If the camper feels that nothing but punitive measures are forthcoming, he will resist. It may be necessary to indicate the probable reasons for his behavior to him so he can properly understand his own motivation.

Every effort should be expended to encourage him to develop self-control and here is another area that can be entrusted to Christ. If there are associates in the camp that have been contributing factors to his problem, make certain each person is confronted and helped. Seek to keep the detrimental influences separated.

Periodic checks on the camper's behavior and relations with others may be necessary, but must be done in a spirit of helping and support, rather than of suspicion. If others in the group are affected, let them know that the situation has been handled and those involved properly corrected.

The assistance of the group may have to be cultivated in order to ensure the proper atmosphere in the cabin and to support or help the camper in question. Any materials taken or used should be restored and repaid. In some instances, the camp director may ask the parents to come to camp and discuss the matter. Any discipline or corrective measures should be meaningful to the camper. Your goal in this should be one of benefit and one that is constructive.

Language is another concern, foul language and swearing is not tolerated at Christian camps. When you run abruptly into this, the typical response is to react quickly, definitely, and let the person know this is not acceptable. Furthermore, one more time will be his undoing! This usually succeeds in stopping the outbursts, but the camper will just be a little wiser and more careful about the next instance and there will be one—you can count on that! Campers expect this and when confronted, it makes little impression upon them because they have experienced this reaction before.

One counselor had a unique way of dealing with the problem. One day, he came upon a couple of campers talking and they weren't aware of anyone else in the vicinity. Their language was rich with descriptive adjectives and four-letter words. The boys looked up as the counselor approached and he smiled and said, "Hi fellows," and they replied rather hesitantly and sheepishly, "Hi." "By the way," the counselor said, "I couldn't help but overhear you as I walked up and I was wondering if you could tell me what those last two words mean." The boys looked a little surprised and stammered out, "Er, uh, what words?" "Oh, you know which ones. I've heard a number of fellows use them and I just was wondering, since you used them if you could tell me what they mean. Most people know what a word means when they use it." "Well, uh, well we just said them I guess. I don't know if we thought what they meant or anything. I guess it's because other guys use them and we didn't think anyone else would hear us."

These two boys were a little taken back as they were confronted in a much different manner about their abusive language. This counselor had used this technique many times and found that it opened the door to discussions as to why a person uses foul language. He wins a hearing when the campers realize that they're not going to be scolded and lectured about what they have done. They find that they can talk with someone about the reason for using the words.

Words that refer to sex or the sexual relationship in some way are often used with complete misunderstanding and misinformation about them. The ensuing conversation, if built upon the above approach, can lead into a very natural and profitable discussion about sex and many of the misconceptions can be cleared up.

In any of the problems concerning swearing or abusive language, the Scriptures can be brought into focus to help the camper find the solution to the problem and the clear presentation of God's view of sex, as presented in the Scriptures. This can be shared so that wholesome and correct attitudes concerning sex can begin or be reinforced.

It isn't uncommon to find that children or teenagers can give us insight concerning proper ways of working with them. Consider these suggestions from the lips of a child.

MEMOS FROM YOUR PLAYGROUND CHILD

1. Don't be afraid to be firm with me. I prefer it; it makes me feel more secure.
2. Don't let me form bad habits. I have to rely on you to detect them in the early stages.
3. Don't make me feel smaller than I am. It only makes me behave stupidly "big."
4. Don't correct me in front of others if you can help it. I'll take much more notice if you talk quietly with me in private.
5. Don't make me feel that my mistakes are sins. It upsets my sense of values.
6. Don't always protect me from the consequences. I need to learn the painful way sometimes.

7. Don't be upset when I say "I hate you." It isn't you I hate, but your being a symbol of authority.

8. Don't take too much notice of my small complaints. At times they bring the attention I need.

9. Don't nag. If you do, I shall have to protect myself by appearing deaf.

10. Don't make rash promises. Remember that I feel badly let down when promises are broken.

11. Don't forget I cannot explain myself as well as I should like. That's why I'm not always accurate.

12. Don't tax my honesty too much. I am easily frightened into telling lies.

13. Don't be inconsistent. That completely confuses me and makes me lose faith in you.

14. Don't put me off when I ask questions. If you do, you will find that I stop asking, and seek my information elsewhere.

15. Don't ever suggest that you are perfect or infallible. It gives me too great a shock when I discover that you are neither.

16. Don't tell me my fears are silly. They are terribly real and you can do much to reassure me if you try to understand.

17. Don't ever think it is beneath your dignity to apologize to me. An honest apology makes me feel surprisingly warm toward you.

18. Don't forget I love experimenting. I couldn't get on without it, so please put up with it.

19. Don't forget that I can't strive without lots of understanding, but I don't need to tell you, do I?*

*Adapted from material submitted to Mrs. Papworth by Dr. Woolitz, Principal, Loma Portal Elementary School. Distributed by Adult Education Department, San Diego Schools.

What a Case!

Chapter 8

Genuine development and growth in camp counseling comes only through the process of actual counseling as you come face to face with the camper and encounter him in a real and honest interpersonal relationship. However, don't be hesitant and fearful of realizing your fullest potentiality as a counselor because of lack of experience and knowledge. As a counselor, you will develop insight and objectivity as you grow more confident in the camping situation.

Preparatory work for camp will take hours of involvement. This isn't work that falls just at the reading level, however. Seek opportunity to exercise your counseling skills and discuss your feelings of frustration, as well as elation with other counselors or church or camp leaders.

You need the feeling of an actual counseling situation and the confrontation of a major discipline problem, the feeling and practice of using the Scripture in leading a person to Christ, and of leading a cabin group discussion and devotions. This section of the book will attempt to deal with this problem by giving guidelines, case studies and situations for practice. The cases presented here are true, with the names of individuals and camps changed.

The first step to understanding campers is to understand yourself. You need insight into your own life—your motivations, fears, feelings, needs, desires, interests and attitudes. In addition, you must learn how to handle these in yourself before you are capable of helping others.

As you read the cases presented here, there are several items to look for and consider.

(1) First of all, read the case several times. (2) Consider the problem. Identify it or indicate if there is more than one problem. (3) What are the feelings that may be expressed or contained? What do you think are the needs of each person here? Why does he act in that way? (4) How do you feel toward the people in the case? Why do you react toward them in that manner? Who do you like and dislike? (5) Is there any possible way that the problems may have been prevented? (6) How would you deal with the problem? What are the

possible solutions and alternatives? What action would you take or whose assistance would you seek? (7) Is this a typical situation that may come up in your camp? (8) What do you think the reaction of the other members of your training group or counseling group will be? Can you see why you attempt to deal with the problem in the manner in which you do? Will your method be successful? Hopefully, your answers will be discussed, shared and reacted to by the others as the insight gathers from involvement with others. This will be of great benefit to all.

BASIC QUESTIONS IN CAMP COUNSELING

1. What are some of the interpersonal problems that may arise between counselors?

2. As you check the beds in your dorm, you find that a camper has a problem with enuresis. You've asked the campers to let you know if this was a problem but there was no response. What are the steps that you would take? Who would you consult and how would you confront the person?

3. Several members of your dorm are teasing a camper because of a stuttering and speech impediment. How would you react to those teasing and how would you counsel with the camper?

4. One of the fellows in your dorm is very effeminate. Several remarks have been made about this person by the other fellows and some of the girls. You've even overheard a couple of the other counselors talking about him. Should you attempt to handle the problem yourself or should you seek

assistance? If so, to whom will you go? How would you react to the other counselors?

5. On the first day of camp, you've noticed a camper who stands off by himself and appears lonely. How should you approach this person and what might be the problem here?

6. One of the girls in camp came running into the chapel and sobbed, "I'm just no good. No one can forgive me for what I did. Can't someone help me, please?" Would you approach this camper immediately with some Scripture? Would you attempt to have a woman counselor talk to her? What would you do with other campers who are there talking to you at that time?

CASE 1

Two high school boys were sitting by one of the trees as their counselor came toward them. As he approached, he overheard one of them say, "That camp director is the worst guy I've ever seen. He talks about being a Christian and then he kicks us out of camp." As Ralph, the counselor, came up he said, "What seems to be the problem, fellows? You sure look down in the mouth about something." Al piped up and said, "You know what that camp director did? He kicked us out of camp and just because we went in to tell him that these guys from the other cabin started a fight with me and they tore my shirt. This camp sure is a gyp, and that camp director—I know what I'd like to do to him." As the story proceeded, it seems that both of these boys had been involved in a minor fracas with five other larger boys and in the ensuing discussion and scuffle, Al's shirt was torn and he was pushed around.

When the others left, these two headed straight for the camp director's office. By the time they arrived, they were going at full steam and without knocking, they barged right into the director's office and found him talking with some of the other campers. According to the boys, he asked them to wait outside until he was through, and then he would talk with them. As the boys went out, they commented, "Man, I sure want to fix those guys that roughed us up. Wait till we tell him."

As soon as they were seated outside the door, the camp director rushed out quite angry and told the boys to go directly to their cabin and pack their bags as they were leaving camp right then and there.

As Al told the story, he said, "He came out and I've never seen him mad like that. He said that we called him a snotty old man and he wasn't going to take that from any campers and we had to leave camp! But we didn't say anything like that, Ralph. Really we didn't! We just wanted to tell him about the fight and my shirt!" By this time, Al and his friend were so upset they were almost in tears. Ralph answered, "Before we go any further, why don't we go back and talk to him again. Perhaps there was just a misunderstanding. As your counselor, I'd like to hear both sides of the story and then we can see what our director thought you said to him, all right?"

John, the boy who had been sitting quietly, responded, "Ah, he doesn't want to see us. He said he was calling our folks and we were going straight home and that was that. He told us not to come back there and . . ." Ralph replied, "Let's give it a try. It won't hurt anything, and I'd hate to have you boys sent home if this is just a misunderstanding."

He finally succeeded in convincing the boys to accompany him to the camp director and as they approached, Ralph knocked on the door and heard the director respond, "Come in." They went in and the director looked up in surprise to see the boys with Ralph. Ralph started out and said, "I ran into the boys outside and they told me what had happened and I thought, well, maybe I could find out what happened."

The camp director flushed a bit and started by saying, "I've never been approached like that before in all my years at camp, Ralph. It wasn't the matter of them rushing into the office, but after I asked them politely to remain outside until I had finished, they called me a mean old man and I didn't see any reason for that! No smart aleck camper should talk to any staff member like that." Al blurted out, "But we didn't call you that. We didn't say anything like that." By this time Al was angry and almost yelling. "These big guys were picking on us and tore my shirt and we came here to tell you about it and that's all we were talking about. Then you come out and jump on us and say we said something that we didn't."

The camp director angrily replied, "Now listen fellows, I heard what you said and it wasn't very polite. You had no call to say that about me and if that's your attitude, you're going home right now.

You know better than to speak to someone like that. I heard you call me an old man and I don't see that you had any reason to do that." John said, "But you just didn't hear us right. We didn't say that. You just don't want to believe us. You're against us too, like those other guys were."

Questions: As you continued in this situation, how would you proceed? There are angry feelings on both sides now. How would you attempt to bring some sense of order to the discussion? Is this your responsibility as a counselor? Who might be at fault here and how could you bring this into the open? Has anything been said that might indicate these fellows have had some other problem? Should you have come to the director alone or was this the best approach? Would this affect your relationship with the director and what are the possibilities? How will this affect your relationship with the campers?

CASE 2

The meeting had started and the last of the campers was scurrying to find his place. Two counselors, Janice and Joane, were standing at the back looking over the group to see if they could assist some in finding a place to sit. The pianist had begun to play and a rousing chorus was being sung with a great deal of enthusiasm.

As the two counselors stayed toward the back of the room, one of the campers came in obviously out of breath, and as she looked for a place to sit down, she noticed the two counselors in the back. She walked up to them and said, "Guess who I just saw walking toward the woods—Carol and Jim. I think they're ditching the meeting. They were sneakish about it and looking back to see if anyone saw them. Boy, wait until I tell the others." Before she could leave, Janice caught her and said, "Sandy, why don't you let us go and find out what is happening out there and let's not mention this to anyone. I think it would just disturb some of those here in the meeting and we don't really know yet if they're the only ones involved, do we?" "No, I guess not. I'd sure like to tell someone, but I'll go sit down and wait until I see you later," said Sandy.

The two counselors looked around the room for the counselors of the two campers mentioned. They finally spotted them, but they were seated in the midst of the meeting hall with campers all around them. They decided that it would be better not to cause a commotion by asking them to leave and decided to go looking for the campers themselves. As they left the room, Joane mentioned to Janice, "I don't see how Mary can put up with that girl in her cabin. She's always up to something and now this. You know with her reputation . . ." "Yes," replied Jan, "and he's no angel. His counselor mentioned that he's tried to ditch every meeting and makes no response at all during cabin devotions. Remember this morning, he's the boy that he asked the other counselors to remember in prayer."

The two counselors hurried toward the wooded area where the two campers were last seen. As they approached the area, they couldn't see the campers anywhere and continued to search the area. As they went down the ravine they rounded the bend and almost stumbled upon the two campers. They scrambled to their feet and looked very surprised and sheepish. Both appeared to be very embarrassed and just stood and looked at the counselors.

Questions: What are some of the implications of what occurred here? What should be done? How should the counselors approach this situation? Would it help to have anyone else be involved as they talk together? To what extent should another counselor be involved in a corrective situation with another counselor's camper when the counselor is inaccessible? Would you involve the men's or women's dean in this situation? Should the women counselors have taken a man counselor with them? What are some of the positive factors that could arise from this situation?

CASE 3

As Jim, the new counselor, came into the cabin, he greeted the high schools boys in a friendly manner. Their response was anything but friendly and the best remark was a gruff, "Hi there" and "Are you our counselor?" It was anything but a warm reception but Jim was determined to really get to know these boys and try to lead them to the Lord during this week at camp. He knew that these were the fellows who didn't attend church and had come to camp because of their girl friends. Their reason for being there was definitely not for the spiritual rewards!

As Jim moved from fellow to fellow asking their names and shaking hands, he noticed that most of them were sharp, clean looking young men. It wasn't long before one of the fellows turned to the counselor and said with a grin, "Hey, I heard this was the type of camp that tried to convert ya. Man, are they going to have a job gettin' me to be religious!" At this, all the other fellows hooted and laughed. The boys in the cabin started to talk among themselves and seemed to ignore Jim.

Every now and then as Jim straightened his bunk and belongings, he heard a number of four-letter words, and the profanity from the fellows increased the more they talked. Occasionally, one of them would look over toward him working at his bunk to see what type of reaction was coming. The language continued and seemed to be a part of the conversation.

This was the pattern of speaking for these boys. Jim continued to work at his bunk and the language deteriorated rapidly into the vulgar vein. In fact, it was so loud and noticeable now that he was sure the fellows and counselors in the other cabins could hear.

Questions: What is really happening here? What is this behavior expressing? What are some other ways that campers can "test" a counselor? What fears and anxieties do you think Jim has because of being a new counselor? How might he react because of lack of experience? How serious is this problem of language? This is the normal behavior pattern for these boys. How would you attempt to approach them about this? Would you ask for assistance with this problem? Would you handle this differently with junior high and junior-age campers, and if so, how? How important is the initial handling of this situation? Should this problem be ignored to see if it might go away, or must every problem be tackled in the initial stages so it doesn't get out of hand?

CASE 4

The evening was warm and the junior-age boys in the cabin were restless, even though they had been active all day. Jim, their counselor, was sure that they would drop right off to sleep because of the day's activities. The devotions had gone particularly well this evening with several of the boys participating and sharing. Even the more reserved fellows prayed tonight.

The lights had been out for about five minutes and from time to time, Jim heard a few snickers from the other side of the dorm, and the rustling of paper. He let this slide by for about ten more minutes and then said, "O.K. guys, it's late and we want everyone to knock off the noise and go to sleep, O.K.? We've got a big day tomorrow." The noise diminished and Jim settled down for some rest, but in a couple of minutes several of the boys burst out laughing and in no time, every boy in the room was contributing to the uproar.

Jim was out of bed in an instant and switched on the light and said, "That's about enough out of all of you. The next boy that makes a sound is really going to get it. Now quiet!" The silence was deafening. Not a peep out of any of them. Jim stood there for a minute and then said, "Thank you," and turned out the light and went back to bed.

The silence lasted almost until he was settled and then someone snickered and the entire dorm exploded in laughter. Again, Jim hopped out of bed and switched on the light.

Questions: Do you think this is a spontaneous situation or could the boys have planned something like this together? Would this make any difference as to how you would handle the problem? What is the best way to handle a problem such as this? Was Jim correct in his approach so far? Which of the following would have been a helpful procedure to follow?

(1) Threaten to take the boy or boys to the camp dean or director.

(2) Have the boy who instigated the action stand outside for five minutes.

(3) Have those involved do twenty pushups to let them know that you do want them to fall asleep. This would help to tire them out even more.

(4) Ask the boys as a group what they think they should do and have them discuss the possibilities and consequences.

CASE 5

Mary was counseling at camp for her fifth year. Next year she would be graduating from college and as she reflected back on the past five summers, she felt that she would really miss camp. Her reverie was soon disrupted when Marcia came into the cabin and flopped on her bunk.

"Hi Marcia, how about walking up to the meeting with me? It's just about that time, you know."

Marcia looked over at her and then turned back to the book she had started to read and didn't say anything. Mary was puzzled by this as Marcia had been a perfect camper for the first two days of camp. She was cheerful and cooperative and had a real wit about her. Mary stood up and walked to the door, "Come on Marcia, we don't want to be late." Marcia looked up and said, "I'm not going to the meeting, Mary."

There was silence for a moment and Mary walked over to the bunk and said, "Why not, Marcia? I thought you were enjoying the camp and the meetings, and well, just everything here." Marcia kept her nose in her book as though she were trying to avoid an answer, but she could sense her counselor standing and waiting for an answer. "I like the camp and all that, and even the meetings, but I just can't go to them any more. Please don't take it personally and please don't make me go to them. I just can't!"

Mary sat down on a chair next to the bed and asked, "Well Marcia, you must have a good reason for not wanting to go. Why don't you tell me about it? I'd like to hear your reason and perhaps I can help in some way." Marcia looked at her and then said, "Well, if you must know, I go to a different church back home and when Sandy told me about the camp, she said it'd be a lot of fun with sports and swimming and meeting some cute boys. She didn't say anything about the meetings and studying and Bible. I like it O.K. but my church wouldn't approve. I can't go to another type of church, and my Mom doesn't know it's a church camp either!"

Questions: Faced with a situation such as this, should Mary attempt to work this out by herself or seek assistance from the camp director? Demonstrate how you would continue this conversation and some of the goals you would have as you proceeded. Is this the type of situation where you would ask the girl who invited Marcia to help you in your counseling? How do you feel about Sandy at this point? Assuming you have tried to talk with Marcia about her church's beliefs and teaching, what would be her probable reaction to you? Indicate what Scriptures you might use as you continue this discussion, and how would you use them or for what purpose?

CASE 6

The two counselors walked slowly up the hill toward their cabins talking about the evening. "That was a message that really got through to some of those girls tonight. I sure wish more of the fellows would respond like that," said Dan. Before Ron, the camp's senior counselor could reply, seven boys descended upon them talking excitedly, and obviously upset. So many were talking that no one could understand a word and Ron had to almost yell before he could be heard. The boys finally calmed down and one of them proceeded to tell what had happened. "Wait until you see the cabin. Oh boy, were we hit hard. We walked into our dorm and it was a mess. It's terrible!" Dan asked, "Well, what's wrong with it? What happened?" The boy who was talking continued, "Someone raided the dorm and we think we know who it was.

There's shaving cream all over the bunks, the mattresses are on the floor, and the sleeping bags in the rafters. They dumped our suitcases, and I bet there's something missing. They stole some stuff from us! You just wait and see! We'll find something missing, and there's pine cones all over the place. We're going to go over to Dorm 8 'cause they did it and, boy, are we going to take care of them."

Ron and Dan both started to talk now. "Now let's wait before you go running off without being sure about the whole situation." Dan had worked with this same group of boys for about three years now. He had been their counselor when they first came to camp in the eighth grade. He knew each boy quite well, including their strengths and weaknesses. He remembered other occasions when they reacted emotionally first and thought later, and the consequences of such action. In fact, one year one of the boys had been sent home because he was uncontrollable.

Ron, at this point, assumed control of the situation and started to question the boys specifically about the state of affairs. "Now, why are you so sure that the boys in Dorm 8 did this? Did any of you see them?" Ken, who had spoken up before, replied, "We didn't have to see them do it. They've been threatening us all week with this dorm raid and now they've gone ahead and done it, and then they had to steal stuff!" All the fellows chimed in at this point and it was a couple of minutes before they were calm enough to proceed.

The questioning continued for awhile and gradually the boys were led to the place where they were ready to return to their cabin with the counselors to survey the damage, and actually determine the extent of missing articles. When they approached the cabin, four of the fellows from Dorm 8 came out and sat on their steps grinning, and just watching. As the boys approached their own cabin, they slowed down and stared over at the other cabin and stopped.

Questions: This situation is fairly common in most camps and a number of avenues of approach have been selected and listed below. Discuss each and attempt to discover the possible outcome of each method, indicating strengths and weaknesses.

(1) Dan took his boys in the cabin and Ron went over to the boys in Dorm 8 and questioned them.
(2) The boys and the counselors surveyed the cabin and then called the camp director to the dorm to let him have a firsthand report and to seek his advice as to how to proceed.
(3) The boys from Dorm 8 were called over by Dan and asked to step into the cabin with everyone else to survey the damage.
(4) All the boys in Cabin 8 were brought together in their own cabin and told that they had been identified as the boys responsible for the dorm raid and everyone would wait right there until the guilty ones confessed.
(5) After surveying the damage, the camp director asked all of the boys in the camp to meet together. During this time, he explained what had happened and asked if anyone had any information concern-

ing the raid. After this, he stated that he would be in his office for the next hour and he would like to have those responsible come to him on their own and discuss what had happened with him.

(6) State how you would have handled this problem. How would you have approached the boys in Cabin 8? their counselor? the camp director? How would you have controlled their boys so a fight didn't develop?

CASE 7

Sandy was speechless as she left the counselor's staff room. She couldn't believe it. It was just too much to believe that Jane and Rich were planning on leaving the camp that night to go into town on a date. Even if this were their first summer counseling, they had as much responsibility as the other counselors and were in charge of a group of campers.

Sandy had found this out quite by accident as she walked into the staff room that afternoon. She had actually been looking for Jane as they had planned to work on their craft program together for the next morning. As she entered the room, Jane and Rich were quietly talking about the time that they would both leave camp and where they would meet. Sandy's face must have registered surprise for as they glanced up and saw her there, Rich said, "Don't look so surprised, Sandy. Haven't you ever cut out for a few hours?" Sandy was taken back and angry. "I haven't and don't intend to, and you certainly shouldn't. You can't leave those campers by themselves. Who's going to look after them, and you know the rules! In fact, we all read and agreed to them before we came. If you sneak off and get caught, they'll send you home. What about your example to the campers!" The more Sandy talked the more angry she became and her voice reflected this.

Jane just sat there and looked at her. She yawned and said, "Sandy, you just wouldn't understand what it's like never getting to be alone with your boyfriend. We're not committing a crime, we're just going to look around town for a little while, and since you know about this, you can cover for me. In fact, I'll even let you look after my girls for me." She finished this statement with a laugh and Rich joined her.

By now, Sandy was boiling and felt it best just to leave the room and think this over. She and Jane had palled around together for years. Sandy had even encouraged her to counsel at camp this summer, but having Rich come to counsel was Jane's idea. Jane's attitude and lack of concern for her campers puzzled and bothered Sandy. She was a conscientious counselor and had a regard for the physical safety, as well as the spiritual condition of her campers.

The big question in her mind now was what should she do? Should she cover for Jane and hope she wasn't discovered? Should she attempt to talk to Jane alone and perhaps have better results than when Rich was around? Should she go to the camp director and tell him the whole thing? What if he didn't believe her? After all, they could deny the whole episode and say that they were just kidding her. What about those campers? What would the parents say about the camp if they found out about the counselors? All these questions raced through Sandy's mind and she wasn't sure what to do. She knew what was right but was in a quandary as how to approach the problem.

The day wore on and following the evening meal, the fireside meeting was held with a wonderful devotion by the camp speaker on "Christian Responsibility." Sandy had difficulty keeping her mind on the subject as she still hadn't reached a solution to the problem. Jane and Rich were sitting among their campers and seemed very attentive and concerned about the message. As the campers dispersed from the fireside area and talked on their way to the snack shop, the two counselors in question talked quietly with one another and then went their separate ways. As Sandy watched Jane leave, she just sat there for a moment wrestling with the decision of what to do. Finally, she bowed her head to ask the Lord's guidance in this matter.

Questions: Sandy was troubled with a question of loyalty here. Should her primary loyalty be to the camp director or policy? the other counselors? or the campers? Sandy raised several questions during her time of distress and uncertainty. Determine the possible outcome for each and the effect it would have on her relation to:

(1) Sandy and Rich
(2) The camp director
(3) The other counselors
(4) The campers

(5) Her own reputation as a counselor and the possible effect upon her future as a counselor.

CASE 8

Mary was a quiet camper. She appeared to be a very sweet and introspective person but was well liked by her dorm mates. Her counselor, Rhoda, however, was concerned because of the apparent lack of response on her part to the Bible study and challenges presented at the evening "Victory Circle" meeting.

On Thursday morning, Rhoda came in a bit late to the general meeting. As she scanned the group of two hundred campers, she was able to locate all of hers except one—Mary. She quickly and quietly asked another counselor if she had seen Mary and the reply was negative. Rhoda slipped from the meeting and went to the dorm and rest rooms to see if she could locate her camper, but she was nowhere to be found.

By this time, Rhoda was worried as this was so unlike Mary.

On the way back to the hall, she stopped at the small Prayer Chapel and noticed someone sitting quietly in the front row. She recognized and approached Mary. "Mary, I've been looking all over for you. I noticed you weren't in the Bible study and searched all over camp. Is anything the matter?" asked Rhoda. "Not really," said Mary, "I've been listening to the Bible study and the speaker all weekend, well . . . it's been very helpful and each time he seems to explain how a person becomes a Christian. I'm not a Christian and I've done some things that have been wrong. Each night I see lots of kids get up and come forward and then come to the Prayer Chapel here to talk with the counselors as they accept Christ and I've really wanted to. Believe me, each night I've wanted to get up and walk forward because I've wanted to become a Christian, but I just didn't have the nerve. I was scared. I want to be a Christian but I wanted to talk with you alone—not with all the others in here. Will you help me become a Christian now?

Questions: Is this a common occurrence that would confront you at camp? How might the counselor have worked with Mary before so that she would have known about her desire to accept Christ? Indicate the Scriptures and the procedure that you would use to lead her or anyone else to Christ. What other procedures would you suggest for a camp to use so campers like Mary would feel more free to indicate their response and make a decision? Because Mary is basically a shy person, how would you counsel her concerning her witnessing as a Christian? Would you encourage her and help to provide an opportunity at camp for witnessing?

CASE 9

John was a real case. He disrupted others at meal time with his shenanigans, he talked and whispered during the meetings, and if someone were goofing off, he was either the instigator or an active participant. From time to time, his actions even repulsed the other campers and turned them against him, but this was no deterrent. His counselor and even the camp director had counseled with him, giving encouragement and positive suggestions.

John came from a Christian home, had been a Christian for six years and was an active member of his church. He was usually instrumental in bringing several others to camp each year and hadn't missed a year himself since he was old enough to attend. Fortunately, his counselor was a person with an overabundance of patience, as many of his deeds had a dampening effect on the meetings. There were occasions when the camp director felt that John should be dismissed from the meetings. Naturally, John was a concern to everyone on the staff and they all prayed for him in the morning staff meeting.

One evening following the last service of the day, John went to the Prayer Chapel and sought his counselor. He was very sincere and the words just tumbled forth. He was very much aware of his behavior and was sorry for the times that he had disrupted the meetings. There appeared to be a sincere motivation on the part of John to change his actions and become a constructive member of the camp, and for a deeper Christian life.

He prayed with his counselor, confessing his sins and telling God that he was sorry and asked for strength to overcome his faults. As they moved from the chapel, they met the camp director and before his counselor could say a word, John blurted the entire story to the director. He seemed very happy and wanted to share this with someone else, and the director encouraged him in his decision. As they stood next to the chapel, the director prayed for him.

During the cabin devotions that night, John didn't participate but for the first time was very quiet. One of the other campers asked what was wrong with him. As the cabin settled down for the night, the counselor felt satisfied and in a way relieved. He again prayed for John before he went to sleep.

By this time the next day, both he and the camp director were very discouraged. John was his old self and even a bit worse. It seemed as though nothing had transpired the night before if one were to judge his actions.

Questions: Should this person have been dealt with in some disciplinary fashion before it had proceeded this far? When a Christian comes seeking to confess sin and desirous of a change in his life, how would you proceed and what Scripture would you use? How important is follow up with a person such as this? Would you have encouraged John to share with his cabin that night? Why or why not? What might have been the outcome? What would be the reason for John's reverting back to a previous pattern of behavior? How would you proceed at this point?

CASE 10

Margaret hesitated a moment when she saw Marie linger behind following the morning devotional hour. Marie wasn't in her cabin, but her counselor had gone on to the cabin and Marie looked as though she wanted to talk with someone.

Margaret went up to her and said, "Hi, Marie, are you going to the dorm?" "No," she answered, "I was hoping to talk with my counselor but maybe you can help me. Last night after the lights were out, I did some thinking, and even though the church I attend back home is very different than the churches that the other kids attend, I decided to accept Christ as my Saviour. I knew what a person had to do because of what the speakers have told us this week, so I prayed to God and asked Christ into my heart." "Marie, that's wonderful. I'm so happy for you," exclaimed Margaret. "Have you told your counselor yet?"

"No, I haven't had a chance. I was waiting here, hoping to see her but I saw you instead. Anyway, it's going to be rough when I get home. My church doesn't allow me to attend a church of another faith or belief and my Mom didn't want me to come up here. She had promised me a trip this year and my Dad won't get a vacation, so she finally agreed to let me come. When I get home, I'm not going back to my church any more. They don't teach about Christ the way they do up here and we never study from the Bible. I'm going to tell my folks that I'm a Christian now and that I'm going to another church. I don't think they will like it much but I'm fourteen years old now and I think I should be able to make up my own mind about something as important as this. Don't you think that's what I should do?"

Questions: Because Marie isn't your camper, should you continue to counsel with her or ask her to talk to her own counselor? Should you investigate her decision and cover Scripture verses with her in order to properly understand her decision? How would you advise her concerning her decision to change churches? What reaction do you foresee if she continues along this line of action? Is this change from churches and possible rebellion from parents indicative of a problem that may exist at home or could it be because of a spiritual change in her life? What Scriptures would you use in dealing with this problem?

CASE 11

Ron had been at camp for several years, but his church attendance was very sporadic and generally he came to church the month before and after camp each year. Janice was very active in her church and her father was the pastor and a leader in her denomination. This was the first year that her church, and for that matter any churches of her denomination, had attended this particular camp.

"Look, my Bible doesn't say that I can't go to this place or that one. I don't know where you get that kind of idea, and furthermore, my church never said that we couldn't attend there." This was the conversation that Jim heard as he came in the snack shop.

Several excited high school fellows and girls were clustered around one of the tables listening intently to three of the group argue. Ron had just finished talking and Janice, the girl opposite him, could hardly wait to continue the argument. "But it's a sin to do things like that. It isn't just my church that says it's wrong. They show us Scripture that tells us that we need to be different than the non-Christians, and even if we don't think it's wrong, the Bible tells us that we should not be a stumbling block to others. What would happen if someone who knew you were a Christian saw you going there? What would he think? Why do you want to go there? Does it do anything for you as a Christian?" Janice was talking very rapidly and gesturing wildly as she talked, and one could sense from the expressions of those around her that some had the same conviction and others held Ron's opinion.

Just then, Ron saw Jim and called over, "Hey Jim, you've got a lot of the answers. Come on over here and straighten out this mixed-up girl. She's got some idea that Christians are a bunch of dead pans and can't go anywhere or do anything and have any fun. I don't find that in my Bible. Go on, tell her what the score is." Before Jim had a chance to respond, Janice turned to him and said, "But Ron," she replied, "a Christian has certain standards and we live a separated life. Why, even our speaker mentioned it for a minute this morning. Do you attend some of the places that Jim's been talking about?"

Questions: Will your answer have an effect upon the campers only, or could there be further considerations in this case? How would you approach this subject, and what would you do about taking sides? Do you know the Scriptures that have been alluded to in this discussion and what Scriptures would you use? How would you approach this if your own philosophy were different than that of the camp philosophy and rules? What is the potential of this for a learning situation, not only for these campers, but for the entire camp? How could this be accomplished—through lecture, role playing, panel, small group discussion, etc? Give reasons for your choice and how you would structure the event.

CASE 12

John was worried when he got out of his bed on the third morning of camp. He was certain that he had heard one of his junior-age campers crying during the night but he didn't know who it was. It was difficult to tell during the black of night and he hesitated disturbing the others in an attempt to find out. Now most of the boys were awake and actively preparing for the day's events. He thought to himself, well, this would be a rather poor time to attempt to find the boy. I'll just have to wait or perhaps the problem will solve itself. He hadn't noticed any of his campers staying to himself or withdrawing. All of them were actively engaged in the meetings, sports program, and craft activities. Perhaps someone had said something to one of the boys and he was brooding over that, or perhaps he had suffered a disappointment during the day. Whatever it was, John hoped that it would work itself out as he had a strenuous day before him.

It was a full day and everything went well for the counselors and the campers. Following lunch and the foolishness around the table, mail was distributed, and this event was eagerly anticipated by both campers and counselors. Letters, and especially packages of cookies, were relished by all. As far as John could tell, letters were received by all of his campers, although he was pretty engrossed in the letter that he had received from his girl friend back home.

As he left the hall, the camp director approached and asked, "Well, John, how are your campers working out for you? Any problems develop with any of them?" John said, "Oh no, nothing to speak of, anyway. They're a pretty good bunch and they sure participate well." "Fine—I'm glad to hear that," replied the director. "You've got a couple of eight-year-olds in there and most of the others have never been away from home before except the Roger brothers. If anything arises, don't hesitate to let me know." "I sure will, and thanks," said John.

The evening passed and lights were out. About an hour after the others were asleep, John awoke to hear the sobs of a boy close to him. He arose and almost bumped into Peter. "Hey there, Pete. What's the problem, something wrong?" Pete continued to cry, and just shook his head. John guided him firmly outside where they could talk so the others in the cabin wouldn't be awakened. "Come on Pete, what's wrong? I'd like to hear about it," asked John. The words stumbled out of Pete, and very brokenly, yet firmly, he replied, "Just let me get out of here. I want to go home—and now!"

Questions: What are some of the reasons for homesickness? Do you see any clue in this case that may have given you insight as to the cause? How would you handle this boy and his problem? Should this behavior be expected with this cabin of campers? Why or why not? How can you use preventive measures so this won't occur? In what way would you improve on the way John handled this situation? What positive signs do you find in John's actions?

CASE 13

This was a winter camp that everyone would remember, and perhaps not just for the positive aspects, either. The lodge that the church had rented for the weekend for its high school group was too small and ill-kept. The dormitory situation was the poorest, as some rooms had space for three or four campers and one large room could accommodate twenty-five. This made it difficult to properly space the counselors.

To make matters even worse, all that was separating the girls' dormitory from the boys' was a swinging door which had been barricaded on both sides.

The problems began the first night when it was discovered that in both the girls' and boys' dorm, several rooms were without counselors. These rooms in particular were very noisy. On the boys' side, one of the counselors who had been assigned to three of these small rooms, simply dozed off to sleep in the midst of the commotion and heard nothing. The discipline and control of his group was left to the counselors in the large room. Needless to say, very few persons managed to get much sleep that night, except the counselors who dozed off on the job.

The real trouble began the next afternoon when several of the boys attempted to raid the girls' dorm. The intentions were harmless and both boys and girls enjoyed the occasion and the ensuing snowball fight that raged between them.

Later, some of the boys appeared with large water guns and buckets of water, and began throwing these through the open doors and windows, and from the roof. Rex, one of the older counselors, realized that the situation was out of hand and stepped in and sought to gain control of the boys. After a few moments, he had most of them together and pointed out the possible consequences of their actions both to themselves, the girls and the property.

As soon as Rex left, a few of the girls began to taunt the fellows and before long, they were at it again. Only this time, the fellows attempted to burst into the girls' dorm from their side through the barricaded swinging door. They had their buckets of water and squirt guns and managed to get most of the girls' dorm and their own soaked.

When Rex came into the dorm, it was obvious that he was angry and upset. He proceeded to bawl out the boys and slowly organized a few of them into a clean-up crew. They had worked for about fifteen minutes when Rex heard someone call his name. He turned around and there stood three of the boys with a bucket of snow and water ready to throw on him. One of the fellows said, "Are you ready for it, Rex?" Rex stood there and replied, "Guys, we've had our fun for the day. It's gotten out of hand and we've got to get this place cleaned up. Now I'm telling you to put that down outside and get in here and help clean up this mess." The leader of the group gave a laugh and said, "You're all dry and you need to get wet like the rest of us. Then maybe we'll help." By this time, Rex had reached his boiling point and before any of the boys could react, he had grabbed the leader of the three in a headlock and forced him to the ground saying, "I told you to drop that and I meant it. You've had your chance and now you're going to shape up."

The boy dropped the bucket and gave him a rough shove and stood up. As Rex stood there, his antagonist jumped to his feet and yelled, "Listen, you ox, you don't have to be so rough. You can clean up your lousy dorm by yourself." With that he shoved open the door and walked out. While the other boys stood around and watched, Rex went to the doorway and yelled, "Come on back in here now and do your share or you'll never go to another of our camps again." Two counselors and several of the girls outside turned and looked at Rex when they heard him yell.

Questions: Do you think that the emotions and feelings that Rex felt were justified? Why or why not? Indicate where Rex and the entire camp staff made their mistakes in this situation. What would you have done to correct each situation in this episode as it arose. Should a counselor ever strike or lay his hands on a camper? What would probably be the outcome of this situation for the campers, the ringleader and this counselor? What effect would this have on the church, the lodge owners and the parents? How might Rex proceed to patch up the problem as it stands now?

CASE 14

"Boy, am I ever tired of sitting," complained Dick. "Yeah," laughed Bill. "I counted how long we had to sit there this morning for the (groan) three meetings—two hours and forty-five minutes. Did you see the schedule that they gave us the first day? Only two meetings in the morning and an hour of athletics. We haven't even been to the athletic field in the morning and now these special seminars or whatever they call them at 4:30! It's gettin' to be too much."

Just then, four other boys came in and one of them asked, "Hey, are you guys with us? We're going to ask Harry about this whole deal of all these meetings. He's counseled here for two years now and I overheard him say he's never been at a camp that's had so much emphasis on meetings. They're cutting us out of two hours of free time." Harry, their counselor, came in and noticed right away that the situation wasn't normal. He looked at a couple of the boys and asked what was going on. The reply was instantaneous. "Harry, what can we do about all these meetings? They told us there would be just so many and that was all right 'cause we know this is a Christian camp. Some of the Bible study they present is good, but we can sit there just so long. They're cutting down on the free time. We're not the only ones who feel this way either. A lot of the gals are griped, too!"

Harry waited a minute before he replied, for he, too, felt as some of them did. The time infraction was actually hampering the program as the campers were becoming restless in the marathon meetings and the messages were lacking in impact because of this factor.

He had been bothered about this for the past day and wanted to talk with his camp director about the problem. He knew, however, before he approached him that he had encouraged the speakers to take all the time they wanted and if they would like to have an extra meeting or two, that was fine. The campers are here to learn, first of all, and some of the other activities must take second place when it comes to the Bible study. This put Harry in a rather difficult position as he sensed the extra meetings were backed by the director and he had a responsibility to the camp policy. At the same time he had his own reactions to cope with as well as that of the campers.

He let his campers continue to talk out their feelings and encouraged them to express themselves by questioning them and helping them to explore not only their feelings, but some of the reasons for the change in programming. Finally, one of them came right out and asked, "O.K., Harry, we've told you how we feel. Now, what do you think about this whole problem and what can you do about it for us? Will you go ask the camp director to watch the time and give us back our recreation program?"

Questions: How would you handle a case where

your own attitude or opinions are contrary to those of the camp policy? Where does your responsibility lie in such a situation? Are these campers justified in their feelings? Why or why not? Could this problem have been avoided with some preventive methods? If so, how? How should you react when your campers react to the camp program or supervisor? Should you ever agree or disagree? What other course of action is left open for you? Is there ever a time when you should go to those in the place of highest authority in a camp and speak for the campers or recommend a change?

CASE 15

Rick could see that the small group of campers were deeply engrossed in conversation as they sat around the towering pine. As he stood there drinking his coke, he meandered toward the boys and could see that they were enjoying themselves by their spontaneous laughter. Rick really liked this group as they were easy-going and cooperative, and had established a fine relationship the first day. He was well-accepted with this group of campers and they were very responsive toward him and were eager to have him around and participating.

"Hi Rick," a couple of the boys yelled to him as he approached. "You really look and sound like you're having a ball over here," replied Rick. "Yeah," said Don, "Frank here can really spin the stories. They're out of sight. Go ahead and tell him that last one, Frank. It's a riot, and the way you tell it really gives it a punch." Frank looked a little sheepish and said, "Ah, I don't know if he wants to hear it or not. Besides, you've heard it once and I won't get any laughter out of it besides Rick. Man, if I'm going to tell a joke, I want an appreciative audience." Most of the boys laughed at this and they encouraged him to tell Rick the story.

Rick found a place where he could lean against the tree and Frank began to talk. As the story developed, Rick sensed that the story wasn't the type that he had expected to hear. He was even dubious as the joke progressed from double meanings to out-and-out profanity and vulgarity. The other fellows sat there grinning and enjoying themselves and Frank was very wrapped up in what he was talking about. Frank gave the punch line and once again, the campers roared and howled with laughter and glee. Frank looked over at Rick.

Questions: When smutty stories or dirty jokes are told in the presence of the counselor, what is the best way to react? If this story or joke were told by a junior-age camper, how would you react? junior high? high school? What type of teaching situations could this lead to and how would you proceed? What would be the advantage of overlooking and ignoring this type of joke? What are the possible results? Is this a situation where you would immediately quote Scripture to the campers and emphasize that "this is a Christian camp and we don't tell those types of stories here"?

CASE 16

The day had been strenuous for campers and counselors alike and Dave was mighty glad to see his bunk. He had already planned his devotions and they would be brief tonight as his main interest right about now was sleep! By the time lights-out rolled around, all of the junior high campers assigned to him were ready for bed and ready for devotions.

Dave was a bit disappointed with the response of some of his campers as they were hesitant to enter in the discussion and sharing time that comprised the evening devotional period. In a way, he was glad that he could finish the devotions in a hurry tonight. As soon as they finished a round of prayer, Dave settled down to sleep, or so he thought.

"Hey Dave," he heard someone whisper, "can I ask you a personal question?" Dave replied, "O.K. go ahead." "You've gone out with girls before. Have you ever kissed any?" Dave answered, "Well, er . . . yeah, I have a few times. Why do you ask?" Jim, the boy who had been asking said, "Oh, some of us have been wondering about it. Not so much that you have but what it's like and, oh you know, what you do after that."

By this time, Dave started to suspect that the question that Jim was asking was deeper than it first appeared. He could see in the dim light that most of the boys were sitting up waiting for his answer. Finally, Dave answered, "You mean, you guys want to know about sex and what it is?" Several of them replied in the affirmative. Dave went on, "Well, haven't you learned something about this in your science and gym classes at school, and what about your home? Your folks have talked to you about this by now, haven't they?" The replies varied from, "naw, not at all," "just a little, but I felt funny when my mom started talking about that stuff, so I left."

One fellow in the group named Bob mentioned that his dad came up to him one day and said, "Bob, it's about time that we had a talk about sex and young boys and girls." So I said, 'Sure, Dad, what do you want to know?'" Most of the boys laughed loud and long to this reply until one of the counselors from another cabin adjoining theirs pounded on the wall and yelled something about lights-out and time to go to sleep. Dave couldn't help but laugh with the fellows at this reply. Bob went on to say, "Yeah, dad never said a thing about that again. He came home with a book another time and said I should read it and all that, but I never did."

By now, Dave was wide awake and wondering how he should proceed. Just then, the counselor from the other side yelled over again and asked them to quiet down. Dave replied to the fellows, "He's right, guys, it's late and we've got to get our sleep." One of the other boys protested, "But Dave, we want to know about this and we don't seem to have a time during the day. There's always some other guys around or worse yet, some girls, and if they heard us talking about this, wow, they'd think we were odd or something. I've heard some of the other kids talk about sex but I don't know if what I heard was right or not, and what about the Bible? It uses some big words now and then that the minister says has to do with sex, but I don't know what all of them mean. Can't you tell us now?"

Questions: The camp has a time for lights-out in the dorms and strives to maintain a set time of rest for the campers. Should Dave continue with the discussion at this time or delay it? What would be the advantages and disadvantages of both methods? Should Dave attempt to handle this or delegate it to someone else on the staff and not discuss it at all? Discuss and adequately explain all of the passages that deal with sex in the Bible and present the biblical view of sex. If you continued the discussion at this time, how would you proceed and how would you deal with the problem of disturbing other campers and counselors who weren't involved in this discussion?

CASE 17

The afternoon sun was very warm and the boys were conscious of its penetrating heat as they trudged along the trail. They had been anticipating this event for several days and for some, it was the high point of their week at camp. They had taken the day to hike to Fern Meadows about nine miles from camp. The trail was well marked, although steep in places, and their arrival at the destination was well worth the tired muscles and dust that they encountered. They had arrived around noon and eaten their lunches and explored the meadow, looking for wildlife and unusual rock formations.

Around two o'clock, they began the trek home. Unknown to Jim, their counselor and the one in charge of this expedition, two of the more adventuresome boys at the end of the line had noticed a stream winding through a narrow gully close to the trail. They thought that they could get to the stream and back without holding up the others or being missed from the group. As they started the descent into the gully, Dick lost his hold and slipped down the incline. His friend Bill saw that he didn't move after he landed at the bottom.

Panic stricken, he rushed up the slope and tore down the trail after the other boys. By this time, however, they had been missed and they were on their way back. Jim was at the head of the line and he could see that Bill was very upset and excited. "Bill, where's Dick? What's happened?" asked Jim. Bill answered between gasps for breath. "He fell and I think he's hurt. Hurry!" The entire group rushed back to the place where Dick lay and they could see from the top of the rim of the gully that he was hurt, although he was conscious.

As soon as he saw them he cried out for help. Jim and three of the older fellows made their way to where he lay. "My leg is twisted and it hurts when I move it. Can't you help me?" cried Dick. "O.K.," said Jim, "just hang on here and let's take a look at it. Can you move it at all? Just where does it hurt?" Dick had quieted down now and in a calmer voice said, "It hurts every time I move it. I think it's broken." Jim thought for a moment and said, "I think the best thing to do is just leave you here and go for help. If it is broken, we can't take a chance moving you and we don't have the necessary equipment to get you out of here and back to camp. I don't know that much about first aid to really know if it's broken or not." One of the other boys piped up. "Hey, we don't need to do that. I've had some first aid and my dad's a doctor. I've seen him set legs before. All we need are a couple of pieces of wood and some cloth and then we can get him out of here without having to go back for help."

Jim was definite, "No, thanks anyway, Pete, but we shouldn't attempt anything like that. We could hurt him worse than he is now." "But Jim," argued Pete, "I've seen it done a dozen times. We'd better do it ourselves. You might not get back before dark and then we'll get him out of here tonight. He'll freeze up here. We've got to take the chance."

Questions: This is a situation that could occur at any type of camp and counselors must be prepared for emergencies. What would seem to be the best course of action here if you were the counselor? Give the reason for your answer. Should all counselors be given some training in first aid for emergencies such as this? What about treating illness back at camp? If you have the training, wouldn't it be easier for you to proceed instead of bothering the camp nurse? If you were the counselor and had received first aid training, should you attempt to handle the problem? Who should make the return trip to camp? Who would be left in charge if you went? Should you go by yourself? Discuss your feelings if you had been the boy with the broken leg and you had listened to the above discussion between Pete and the counselor.

APPENDIX

TALKS FOR CABIN DEVOTIONS

Juniors

FIRST DAY Saved and Lost

Read Luke 15:2-6 Page 162 in "The Man Jesus"

There is a word we hear a lot around camp. It is the word, "saved." What do you think it means to be saved? (Wait for comments. Do not add any of your own at this time. Follow this procedure with all the questions.)

There is another word that goes right along with it. The word is "lost." That word was in the few verses we just read. What does it mean to be lost? Here at camp it is easy to think about being lost on a trail. What does this mean? You know you are where you are, that's no problem. What is the problem is that you don't know how to get where you're going. Now isn't that the problem of the sheep in the Scripture we just read? He knew where he was but he didn't know how to get to the shepherd. So the shepherd came and found him. The sheep let the shepherd pick him up and take him back to where he belonged. Now the sheep was saved.

Let's get back to you. You are lost when you don't know how to get to Jesus Christ. You can't find the way, so the Lord Jesus, the Good Shepherd, comes and finds you. Now, you are saved when you ask the Lord to forgive you for sinning and let the Lord Jesus be your Shepherd and follow him.

SECOND DAY Born Again

Read John 3:1-8 Page 30, "The Man Jesus"

Last night we talked about two words that we hear around camp, "saved and lost." Tonight in our Scripture there were two more words that may not sound so hard, and yet we better be sure we understand. What do you think the Lord Jesus meant when he said, "born again"? (Wait for comments.) If we take the phrase apart, "born" means to start life, and "again" means a second time. Then, we could say that "born again" means to "start over," or better yet, "to start life over." That's not a bad idea, is it? Get away from the mistakes and the failures and start over. Well, when you become a Christian, that is just what you do, "you start a new life," you begin all over again.

Now, maybe you don't feel like that fits you. You may not feel that everything is that different, but everything is different. Can you guess how? (Wait for comments.) Before you became a Christian you had one father and you were the member of one family. After you become a Christian you have God as your Father and you are the member of two families. (Read John 1:12.) You are a child of your earthly father, and you are also a child of God. And that's what it means to be born again.

THIRD DAY How Can I Be Sure?

Read John 10:22-30 Page 156, "The Man Jesus"

The verses which we just read include the answer to the next question we're going to think about. We thought about what the words "saved and lost" mean, then talked about the words, "born again." Now, tonight we are going to think about this question, "How can I be sure that God has really saved me, that I have really been born again?" What is your answer? Are you sure? How? (Wait for comments.) What helps do our Scripture verses give us? Let's look at them. The Lord is calling us sheep, isn't he? And he says, "My sheep recognize my voice." When you recognize someone, you know who he is. Do you know who Jesus Christ is? (Let them tell you.) He is the Son of God, our Saviour and Lord.

Then, our verses say, "I know them." Jesus Christ knows you. And do you see what else he says? "I give unto them eternal life and they shall never perish." That reminds me of another verse. Do you know which one? Let's repeat John 3:16 together. There is the same phrase, "anyone who believes in him will not perish but have eternal life." To believe in Jesus Christ, means to recognize who he is, to ask him to be your Saviour and to cleanse you from sin. Now, if you have done this—believed in Jesus Christ—God says in his Word, he will give you eternal life—he will save you. God cannot lie. If he says he gives you life and saved you, he does!

FOURTH DAY What Do I Do If I Make a Mistake?

Read Luke 22:54-62 Page 242, "The Man Jesus"

The story of Peter's denial of the Lord Jesus always makes me stop and think. I'm sure Peter didn't mean to sin but he did. We don't sin because we mean to. Usually we get caught in a bad situation just as Peter did, and before we know what's happening, we do the very thing we know we should never do. The question tonight is, "What should you do when you make a mistake?"

We are thinking tonight about Christians who sin. We have already talked about what a person should do to become a Christian.

Peter was very sorry that he had sinned. What did he do? (He wept.) But being sorry is not enough. The Bible gives the answer. (Read I John 1:9, or, if the juniors know the verse repeat it together.) What does the verse mean, "confess our sins"? It means to tell God that you sinned and that you are sorry and that you want him to forgive you. If you do this, what will he do? (Help the campers to see that the rest of the verse is the answer.) How do you know the Lord will forgive you and cleanse you from sin? The answer is really the same as, how do you know that God saves you. Because he says so! We can always be sure that what God says is true.

FIFTH DAY What Does God Expect of Me?

Read John 15:1-5 Page 229, "The Man Jesus"

The Lord Jesus had a very important truth to tell the disciples. He wanted to be sure that they would understand and so he told by giving them an object lesson. We read in our Scripture, now let me tell it to you in my own words. The Lord said, "You men are my followers." Now, I'm going to say it just for us. You campers who have said that you want the Lord Jesus to be your Saviour are the followers of Christ. In fact, you are more than followers, you are getting this new life of yours right from the Lord Jesus himself. Take a look at a tree or a bush or anything that is growing around here. See the branches. Where does the branch get its life? That's easy, from the tree. Suppose I break the branch off and hold it in my hand, will it still grow? Of course not! Why? Because it has been separated from the tree. "Well," the Lord said, "you are branches, I am the tree or the grapevine. If you want to live and grow and bear fruit you will have to stay with me. If you are separated from me, you will not grow and you will not bear fruit." Now, isn't that simple?

Well, let's say, "It's easy to understand, but not always easy to do." The Lord Jesus said that this staying close to him was "abiding." In verse 10 he told how to abide. "Keep my commandment," or obey God. That's the secret, and that's what he expects of you.

SIXTH DAY A Wise Man

Read Matthew 7:24-27 Pages 64 and 65, "The Man Jesus"

In these verses the Lord Jesus described a wise man. What did he say? (Wait for comments.) There are two parts, aren't there. First, "listen" then "follow" or "obey." Do you want to be a good disciple of Jesus Christ? Then this is for you.

How do you listen? (If no comments, amplify as follows.) In school you are learning to listen, aren't you? You hear a record or a tape or see a TV program or your teacher talks to you. You are quiet, that's one of the requirements for listening. You pay attention, that's another. If you apply these thoughts to your Christian life, how do you listen to God? (You are quiet and you pay attention.) To what, do you pay attention? How does God speak to you? The best source is the Bible. You may not understand everything in the Bible. But when you really listen, you will be amazed at how much you do understand. There are many times when the Bible words are so simple and plain that you will have no trouble at all knowing what they mean. Start with the parts you do understand, and don't worry about the hard parts.

What is the other thing that a wise man does beside listen? (He obeys or follows.) Listening is the first part. You'll have to do that to know what to do. The second part is just as important: when you know what God wants you to do you are to do it. And these two things qualify you to be called a "wise follower of Christ."

Junior High

FIRST DAY Where Am I?

Read Luke 15:10-24 Pages 163 and 164 in "The Man Jesus"

This is such a familiar story that sometimes we listen to the words without really thinking about what they are saying. Let's try to get a fresh look by putting ourselves in the story.

If the Lord Jesus were telling the story today and you were the younger brother, he might say it something like this: A man had two sons. One day the younger went to his father and said, "I'm growing up, I'm in junior high now. I would like you to think of me as old enough to make my own decisions. So, if you will just give me a free hand, I'll live my own life and do as I please." His father agreed and gave him what he wanted.

Now, the junior high was an average young person: he made a few mistakes, he lived mainly for himself, forgot about his family, disobeyed the commands of God, made the wrong friends, a few things like that. He got pretty disgusted with himself, but he hated to admit he had failed.

Let me stop the story right there for a minute. This is the picture of any of you, who does not know Jesus Christ as his own Saviour. The story is pretty bad if it ends there. But this is a special kind of story, each person can write the ending as he chooses. Where are you? That's up to you. You can stay right where we left the junior high, disgusted and pointless, or you can continue the story and come to God and ask him to forgive you for Jesus' sake and make you his child. It is entirely up to you.

SECOND DAY Who Am I?

Read Luke 15:3-7; Matthew 18:11-14; Luke 12:6,7
Pages 162, 116, 149 in "The Man Jesus"

I like these verses that we just read. There is something about them that always makes me feel comfortable. I think the point is that here are the assurances that somebody cares about me. Did you notice that? When one sheep was missing the shepherd cared enough to go and look for it.

In the first story about the sheep, the shepherd called all of his friends in to celebrate with him when the one sheep was found. In the second story the shepherd was talking about children and he said that each one was important to him and that not one should perish.

Then in the last two verses that we read, the Lord Jesus said that God cares for the sparrows and that each person is of more importance than a sparrow. He said that he knows all about each one of us, he even knows how many hairs you have on your head. Do you see what I mean? Each one of you is very important to the Lord Jesus. He cares for you and he understands you and he wants you to be his child. I like that. I'm glad to know that God cares that much about me. And he cares that much about you. So the next time either of us gets discouraged and feels that he stands alone and misunderstood, think about these verses. You are not alone when you know Christ. And there is always at least one person who really understands.

THIRD DAY What Should I Get Out of Camp?

Read Matthew 13:1-8; 18-23 Pages 75-77 in "The Man Jesus"

Here is another of the very familiar stories that the Lord Jesus told to the people. Let's take it apart as we did the one of the prodigal son and maybe we can make it plainer, too. I don't think we are wrong if we say that this camp is the field. Our speakers and leaders are the sowers. Each one of us is represented by the kinds of soil the Lord described. You think about it and see which one describes you. There are some, maybe right here in this cabin, who are the footpath. You are not particularly interested in what is being said. You came to camp for the fun and you go to the meetings and classes only because you think you should.

Then, there are others who go and listen and you believe that what the speaker is saying is true. In fact, here at camp, you don't have much trouble being interested and even taking part in the meetings. But, when you get away from camp, back home, gradually you read the Bible less and less, you don't pray as often, you can't seem to find words to talk about the Lord, in fact you don't really want to. This is the stony ground the Lord describes.

The next one is the person who listens to what is being said. You believe it, too. As you sit there you think, you know I'm going to do something about what I believe. You decide that you are going to take some time in the afternoon to think and pray about what God wants of you. But then, recreation and game time comes. You decide to go swimming instead of praying. You decide you'll talk to me or one of the speakers another time. Maybe you thought you'd talk to someone tonight after the last meeting, but it got late, you wanted to go to the snack shop, and now you're just too sleepy to be bothered. Here is the thorny ground Christ talked about.

The last group I don't really have to describe. You can see that the Lord was talking about the sincere Christian who listens and obeys.

Without talking to anyone else, take a few minutes right now and quietly consider where you fit in this picture. Then, let's talk about what we can do about it.

FOURTH DAY What's Wrong with Wanting the Best?

Read Luke 14:7-11 Pages 159, 160 in "The Man Jesus"

These are strange verses that we read tonight. The story is different from any of the others that we have been thinking about this week and it poses a question that should be interesting to think about. What's so wrong about wanting the best? What do you think? (Listen to the comments that the campers make. You will learn a great deal about how they feel and where they need help if you encourage them to speak frankly about their feelings. When the discussion gets into just a rehashing of previous ideas, be prepared to summarize. Include something as follows.)

Really there is nothing wrong with wanting to succeed, is there? This is a good trait. We can't help but be pleased with someone who does a good job. In fact, we are not very good examples for Christ if we settle for less than the best in ourselves. Each job that you take, do the very best you can.

Well then, what was the Lord talking about in the story that we read? The problem was how the man tried to be best. He just took it for granted that everyone would want him to be the most highly honored. See, this is quite different from doing a good job and getting credit for it. This is expecting to have the best of everything just because you like yourself that much. Do you see the difference? It's a very important one to see.

FIFTH DAY If a Person Is Wrong, Why Shouldn't He Suffer?

Read Matthew 18:21-35 Pages 117, 118 in "The Man Jesus"

There is something about the words of the Lord Jesus in this parable that brings me up sharply every time I read them. I guess this business of forgiving people and of not holding a grudge is a part of everybody's life. You have probably heard people say, "Well, I'll forgive him if I have to, but I'll never forget what he did to me." That's the grudge bit, isn't it? Or, sometimes the person says something like this: "Oh, I suppose I'll forgive him eventually, but let him suffer a little first." Then, there are times when we just get so angry at something that has happened that we would rather lose a friend than forgive him.

The Lord Jesus had just been talking about forgiving people and then Peter came up with a question. "Lord, how many times do I have to forgive someone for doing the same thing over and over?" The Lord said, "You just keep forgiving, you don't keep count." Now, what do you think about that? Do we really have to forgive someone who deliberately does something to us? Can we pretend to forgive but keep holding it against him? Suppose the person who has hurt you is a good friend, does that make a difference? Suppose it is a teacher or one of the leaders at camp? Or, maybe a member of your family? Is it hard really to forgive someone? Do you think you have to? Why? (Encourage discussion. Then continue.)

The Lord Jesus didn't leave us any loopholes, did he? He was pretty blunt with Peter and in the story that he told. Yes, we do need to forgive others if we really want to please our Lord. You know, this is something we should pray about. Certainly we will need to rely on the Lord if we are ever to be able to do what he wants us to do.

SIXTH DAY Do You Have What It Takes?

Read Luke 14:25-33 Page 161 in "The Man Jesus"

We read these verses tonight because there is something in them we need to remember, especially as we think about going home. We all know that it is pretty easy to live for Christ here at camp. After all, everyone is thinking about the Lord. All of us remember to have our devotions every day because we have them here together. All day long we are reminded to seek the wisdom of Christ. We have probably prayed more this week than we prayed for the past two weeks put together. But now camp is almost over. We'll be going home tomorrow. We'll be on our own. We'll meet people all day and probably none of them will remind us to read our Bibles and pray. So, you see, these verses are what we need to get us ready for this change.

Did you notice that the Lord said, "Don't begin until you count the cost." What do you think he meant? (Wait for comments. Then continue.) Do you think it really costs to be a Christian? How?

(Let the young people give their ideas.) Let's try to be really practical. If you are a Christian, how do you think it will cost you when you get home? (Encourage ideas. You may have to help by starting off with your own assessment of how it costs you to be a Christian. Be realistic and specific. This will help your junior highs to come to grips with their potential problem spots. Take each answer and discuss what that young person can do to help him in his Christian life. Be specific.)

Well, this brings us to our question, "Do you have what it takes?" If you depend on yourself, no! If you get your strength from the Lord through prayer, Bible study, and asking him to live in you, yes!

High School

FIRST DAY How Good Is Good Enough?

Read John 3:1-21 Chapter 6 in "The Man Jesus"

The point that always amazes me when I read this passage is the way the Lord talked to Nicodemus. I guess the fact that Nicodemus was a good man is what makes the words seem unusual. He was a Pharisee, a ruler of the Jews, a fine upstanding pillar of society. I think he may well have been a self-satisfied pillar of religious society. And yet the Lord Jesus greeted him with a shocking declaration. "Nicodemus, there are going to have to be some radical changes in your life or you are never even going to see the Kingdom of God."

Now that brings me to my question. How good does a person have to be to be good enough? What do you say? (Let the campers give their ideas. Don't disagree or tell them that they are wrong. Make a mental note of what is said and who says it so that you can correct the misconceptions in the general summation at the end of the discussion. Without pointing out anyone specifically bring out the following.) No matter how hard anyone tries, he can never be good enough. One mistake in life disqualifies you. So, the Lord Jesus said, "If you are born again, your past with all its failures is cancelled, and I give you eternal life—my life." This takes care of the question, for Jesus Christ is good enough! You qualify because you are his child. Are you his child?

SECOND DAY Is Anyone Too Bad?

Read John 4:1-45 Chapter 8 in "The Man Jesus"

This story isn't at all like that of Nicodemus, is it? This woman certainly didn't consider that she was good enough. The fact that she was a Samaritan meant that the Jews didn't consider her to be important at all. In fact, did you notice she referred to herself as a "despised Samaritan"? Then, added to her nationality was the problem of her frequent marriages. No, there was no question in her mind; she knew she wasn't good enough. Her problem was, "Because of who I am and what I have done, am I too bad?" What do you think?

It's interesting that the Lord used the word "believe" in both chapters. He said it to Nicodemus, then the woman "believed" that he was the Christ, and the people of the town "believed" on him. Good and bad it seems all come to Christ the same way. Believe in him, put your trust in him and he will save you. It is as simple but as definite as that.

One more point about this story: When the disciples returned they were amazed that the Lord would waste his time talking to a Samaritan. They apparently considered that she was beneath them and certainly beneath the Lord, so why bother with her salvation. Do you see any parallel in this attitude today? (Wait for comments.) Sometimes we get the idea that it is all right for missionaries and professional Christian workers to care for certain people, but we shouldn't be concerned with anyone but our own particular "in-group." I guess that's because it's easier that way, we feel we don't have to get involved. Well, it may be easier, but it certainly is not scriptural. What can you and I do about it?

THIRD DAY Some People Just Don't Understand

Read Luke 4:16-30 Chapter 9 in "The Man Jesus"

This is the first time that we know the Lord Jesus went back to Nazareth after the start of his public ministry. His return started well. He went to the synagogue, was invited to read the Scriptures—everything was looking up. Then came the question about his father. And the Lord answered, "You are probably saying, do something to make us believe you are the Son of God. Perform some miracles." But he would not do what they wanted.

In the next scene the people are attempting to destroy him by pushing him over the brow of a hill. You see, they just didn't understand. That sounds familiar, doesn't it? So many times it seems to us that the people we would think would be best able to help us—our family—are the very ones who don't seem to understand.

Now in the instance in the Bible the whole situation is obvious. We know the Lord is right, the people are wrong. But when we consider specific instances in our own lives, we cannot really be so objective or so positive. There is an old saying that there are "two sides to every story." The truth of the matter is that there are many sides to every situation. It is not so simple that there is just a right and a wrong, a black and a white. The problem for us is how do we cope with a situation when it seems that we and our family or close friends are not communicating. What do you think we can do? (Wait for comments. Then summarize.)

I know it sounds almost too pat, but the only real answer is to commit it to God in prayer. Now, this doesn't mean that either you or those on the other side pray that the opposition will change its minds. It does mean that both of you ask that the Lord will show each of you what he wants you to do.

FOURTH DAY What Difference Does One Person Make?

Read Luke 4:31-44 Chapter 10 in "The Man Jesus"

Do you ever get the feeling that you are just one person in the midst of a mass of humanity? And that what you do does not really matter? Then, let me ask you this about the Scripture we just read: How many of the people in the accounts can you call by name? In fact, those people in Nazareth that we read about last night, who were they? Name one of the people who lived in the city of Sychar where Jesus preached? Or, what was the name of the woman at the well? You see, the Bible is filled with a great many people known only to God. But their story is important.

It is true you may not change the course of history. You may have a hard time filling a scrap-book with your press clippings. But the fact remains, you do make a difference. Now, the question is how? What do you think? (Wait for comments.)

It's so obvious that what you do affects the people around you, even on a small scale of influence, that I'm not even going to talk about it. Forget that part for a minute and consider this: You make a difference to yourself. You have to have some self-respect. You are an individual, God loves you, as a Christian you bear his name, so stand up straight, hold your head high and make your decisions wisely—you are somebody. And what you do makes a difference when you look at yourself in the mirror. Be the kind of a person you would like to know.

FIFTH DAY Is Christianity a Series of "No's"?

Read Mark 2:23-26; Matthew 12:5-14 Chapter 11 in "The Man Jesus"

Here are groups of people who became so mixed up with the rules that they lost sight of life. In their instance it was the question of how the Sabbath should be observed. You see, the Lord Jesus was doing and advocating certain actions and the people believed that he was wrong. For them religion was a matter of keeping a set of rules, and the more they kept the better they thought they were. Do you see anything wrong with that attitude? Do you agree that Christianity is a series of "thou shalt nots?" (Wait for comments. After several have expressed their opinions, summarize and follow along the following lines.)

Sometimes we are guilty of talking about the "way of salvation." We talk about the Christian life as though it were a thing. And we are wrong. Christianity is the relationship between two people, you and God through the Person of Jesus Christ. Christianity is coming to know Jesus Christ personally, as you come to know a friend. It is learning what pleases him by spending time with him. That's how you get acquainted with people here at camp, that's how you get acquainted with Jesus Christ. As you know him better, you know what he likes and you do those things. But the difference is the motivation, you do them because you want to please your friend, not because you have read a list of rules that you must obey or suffer the consequences.

SIXTH DAY Does Anything Go?

Read Matthew 5:33–6:15 Portion of Chapter 12 in "The Man Jesus"

Does it seem that these verses are just the opposite to those we read last night? Here there seems to be a list of rules and just last night we talked about the fact that Christianity is not a matter of rules. What do you make of this? Were we wrong last night. How do these fit in? Maybe we aren't really supposed to do them? (Use questions like those above to help to get the young people to discuss the problem of rules. Then conclude with something like the following.)

You can't live without guidelines or standards. Some of these are set for you by the government, school, society, family and even by you. Stop and think about it for a minute, you have a number of these that are a part of your life every day. You get up in the morning and you shower, brush your teeth, comb your hair. These are standards that you live by. Follow yourself through the day, you have a lot of them. Some are much more far-reaching than others. Some of greater consequence than whether you comb your hair in the morning. Now, the verses that we have just read are guides for establishing important standards. These are some of the principles that God says members of his family are to include in the standards they establish.

Remember rules do not save you. Salvation is a matter of personal relationship between you and Christ. These are the guidelines by which you live after you are a Christian. Every Christian must establish his own standard before God. When the Bible gives direct command, then you know that belongs on your list. There are other instances when you will decide for yourself what you will do about certain questions. But you will have to decide. Christianity is not a matter of rules and "thou shalt nots." But a Christian does have standards by which he has decided he wants to live.

THE TRAINING PROGRAM

Counselor preparation involves time and effort on the part of the camp or church, but it will help to insure a successful camp. Counselor selection should be completed well in advance of the camp so that adequate time is available for preparation.

The purpose of any camp counselor training program is: 1) to acquaint the counselor with the philosophy and purpose of that particular camp, 2) to challenge him to the work and ministry of camping and counseling, 3) to reduce any anxiety and feelings of inadequacy and to handle any questions that the counselor may have, 4) to give some basic experience in the area of actual counseling procedures and situations before the camp gets underway, 5) to learn how to work with campers.

The training approach should be threefold.

1. Reading in the area of camp counseling and camper characteristics.

2. Group discussion with emphasis on personal feelings toward the prospect of counseling.

3. Group and individual involvement in role playing and analyzing of actual camping situations.

READING: This book will serve as an initial beginning in the area of reading as a basic background for camp counseling. An extensive bibliography has been included for the purpose of providing other resource materials. Books in the area of children and adolescent characteristics will help to understand the age group. Other books in the area of counseling, camp lore, camp recreation, camp maintenance and camp programming will give a wider exposure to the total program of camping. This will lead to a deeper appreciation for the camp's philosophy and value of other personnel to the total program.

GROUP DISCUSSION: This will be a supportive and insightful device as counselors seek to alleviate their fears and gain support and understanding of this new ministry—camp counseling. As a group of new or experienced counselors meet together, opportunity for getting to know one another can be provided. Any group needs a feeling of rapport and comradeship before they really function together as a group. When group members feel comfortable with one another, they feel enough at ease to express their inner feelings. The group discussion situation should be structured in such a way that basic questions about the camp and the work can be aired and discussed. These can be answered, not only by the leader, but other contributions from group members will also have merit.

Fears about working with specific age groups, what to do in this or that circumstance, how to cope with a behavior problem, how do I get to know my campers and to whom am I responsible: these are just a sampling of some of the questions that will be raised.

EVALUATION OF CAMP CASES AND SITUATIONS: This will be the most valuable training device that a camp and church can use as it projects the counselor into the actual counseling situation with a minimum of danger for "goofs" in the counseling relationship. The cases presented in the book are for the purpose of actual practice. The questions and cases presented can be handled in the following manner. Counselors can react to the questions on an individual basis and attempt to arrive at a solution. The findings then can be shared with the entire group so that they can be evaluated. Further analysis can take place at the group level. Role playing should be used with these cases as well as other cases and examples that members of the group may contribute.

Role playing is simply a method of human involvement or interaction that involves realistic behavior, but in imaginary situations or past experiences. It is a method of reconstructing past situations and viewpoints for analysis and evaluation by working through them in a simulated life manner. Role playing is not only a training device for the participants, but an information-giving situation for those in the observation role.

The participants learn by doing and the observers learn by watching, analyzing and identifying. It makes a person self-conscious and thus very aware of his behavior and actions and brings them into a new focus. He becomes more sensitive to his actions and the underlying feelings. This in turn helps one to develop a greater sensitivity toward other's feelings and problems.

Another value of role playing is that it is one of the better methods of improving relationships within groups of people and it allows active participation with real problems. Freedom for experimentation is also available without the danger of making mistakes that are detrimental to the other individual involved. By role playing, you have the opportunity to project yourself into the situation of the other person and gain a better understanding of their feelings and attitudes.

As you attempt to set up role playing situations, proceed with a case or situation that is familiar or simple and not too threatening. The person leading the group should be warm and friendly and relaxed as the group will respond accordingly. Select those counselors who are secure and confident as the beginning participants will lessen the threat for the others. As you prepare for the actual role playing situation, the description of the situation should be explained to all present.

Background information can be given and those who will act out the problem can be selected. The role or character given in a specific case will be given to the prospective counselor and they will then proceed to act out the case or situation. The leader should clarify the fact that role playing is different than acting. This is not a test of acting skill. Because the person is going to enact a role, he will need some background or framework out of which to work and proceed. This can be done by the leader giving information, questioning the person as to how he feels he will react and allowing the person to think through his role for a few moments before proceeding with the role play.

One person is selected as the counselor and one

as the camper. The "camper" will present the problem as though it is his very own and will talk in the first person. The "counselor" responds to this person and the role playing is in motion. In many role playing situations, those involved actually interact according to their own personality structure and the role playing becomes real as they become enmeshed in the actual situation.

There are many variations to role playing. Some groups will want to deal with the same case several times and as soon as one member has had the opportunity to approach the "camper's" problem in his way, another may wish to tackle the situation. Perhaps the "counselor" and "camper" will switch roles and attempt to see the problem from another's vantage point and framework. In role playing where just two of the members are involved, the rest of the group would profit from some guidelines as there is a maximum of participation on their part. They can be asked to look for voice changes in the participants, body tension or facial expression and gestures for these express the inner feelings and tensions that are present.

Assumptions and motives can also be observed. Before the observers have an opportunity to comment on what took place, those directly involved should express their own performance and feelings. They may be able to see how they should have reacted or what they should have said and the "camper" can express how he felt when the "counselor" was making a specific statement to him. This helps one to see what he is really expressing and how others hear and interpret us.

The others can be given a list of questions to consider as they observe and evaluate or even a preplanned form which serves as a guide. When the observation group comments, the discussion should be focused on the problem itself rather than the person.

Others may wish to show their constructive suggestions by demonstrating how they would have handled the situation. In crder to draw out the audience or observers, questions such as "What were the reactions to this statement?" or "Was it what was said or how it was said that caused the camper to react in that way?" or "Why did that particular camper's remark bother the counselor so much?" and finally, "What would you have said?" When they desire to tell you what they would have said and done, have them demonstrate.

Much of the value of role playing depends upon the discussion and analysis after the session, and this is somewhat dependent upon the observations of the others. All members of a training group should go through the experience of role playing and this will take time, and perhaps two or three sessions together.

Another approach would be to divide the training group into smaller groups of three. Give each group a typical camp situation, a real case study, or let the members devise their own. One member acts as the counselor, one as the camper and the third as an observer. The camper presents and structures the situation and the counselor attempts to deal with this for about 10-15 minutes.

The session is stopped and the observer presents

his view as to what he saw and felt. The camper discusses his own reactions and feelings. Then the roles are reversed with the camper becoming the counselor and the counselor becoming the camper, and the same or a similar process is repeated. The same discussion procedure is followed and then the observer can switch roles with a member.

To further aid the discussion process, two groups of threes can get together to discuss their experience and then the entire group can share together. This method will deliver information in a way that no other method can do. It will change and develop attitudes. It will deal with fears and anxieties and help to dispel them. It will create a more secure counselor and will create awareness on the part of this person. He, in turn, will be more sensitive in his relationships with others.

BIBLIOGRAPHY

Beck, Helen L.: GOING TO CAMP. New York, Stephen Dave Press, 1950.

Benson, Reuel A., and Goldberg, Jacob A.: THE CAMP COUNSELOR. McGraw-Hill Co., 1951.

Bently, Walter: BRASS TACKS FOR COUNSELORS. 14 Beacon St., Boston, 1940.

Berg, B. Robert: PSYCHOLOGY IN CHILDREN'S CAMPING. Vantage Press Inc., 1958.

A BIBLIOGRAPHY OF CAMP SAFETY, HYGIENE AND SANITATION. New York, National Safety Council.

Bonnell, John: PSYCHOLOGY FOR PASTOR AND PEOPLE. New York, Harper & Bros. Publishers, 1960.

Bowman, Clarice M.: SPIRITUAL VALUES IN CAMPING. New York, Association Press, 1954. $3.00.

Burke, Edmund H.: CAMPING HANDBOOK. Arco Publishing Co., 1955.

Burns, Gerald: PROGRAM OF THE MODERN CAMP. Prentice-Hall, Inc., 1954.

Camp Commission, National Sunday School Association: GUIDING PRINCIPLES FOR CHRISTIAN CAMPING. Chicago, The Association Press, 1962.

CHURCH CAMPING FOR JUNIOR HIGHS. The Westminster Press.

Cole, William: SEX AND LOVE IN THE BIBLE. New York, Association Press, 1959.

Coleman, Frank G.: THE ROMANCE OF WINNING CHILDREN. Cleveland, Union Gospel Press, 1948.

Corbin, H. Dan: RECREATION LEADERSHIP. Prentice-Hall, Inc., 1953.

Cunningham, Ruth: UNDERSTANDING GROUP BEHAVIOR OF BOYS AND GIRLS. Teachers College, Columbia University.

Des Grey, Arthur H.: CAMPING. The Ronald Press Co., 1950.

Dimock, Hedley S.: ADMINISTRATION OF THE MOD-

ERN CAMP. Association Press, 1948.
Dimlock, Hedley S., and Hendry, Charles E.: CAMPING AND CHARACTER. New York, Association Press, 1929.
Dimock, Hedley S., and Statten, Taylor: TALKS TO COUNSELORS. New York, Association Press, 1939.
Dobbins, Gaines S.: WINNING THE CHILDREN. Nashville, Broadman Press, 1953.
Doherty, J. Kenneth: SOLVING CAMP BEHAVIOR PROBLEMS. Association Press, 1944.
Doty, Richard S.: THE CHARACTER DIMENSION OF CAMPING. New York, Association Press, 1960.
Dreikurs, Rudolf: CHILDREN: THE CHALLENGE. Duell, Sloan and Pearce, 1964.
Dreikurs, Rudolf: PSYCHOLOGY IN THE CLASSROOM. Duell, Sloan and Pearce.
Driver, Helen, and Contributors: COUNSELING AND LEARNING THROUGH SMALL GROUP DISCUSSIONS. Wisconsin, Monona Publications, 1958.
Eisenberg, Helen and Larry: OMNIBUS OF FUN. Association Press, 1956.
Ensign, John and Ruth: CAMPING TOGETHER AS CHRISTIANS. John Knox Press.
Frank, Lawrence K.: HOW TO BE A MODERN LEADER. New York, Association Press, 1954.
Gallagher, J. R., and Harris, Herbert: EMOTIONAL PROBLEMS OF ADOLESCENTS. New York, Oxford, 1958.
GOOD COUNSELORS MAKE GOOD CAMPS. #19-530, Girl Scouts.
Goodrich, Lois: DECENTRALIZED CAMPING. Association Press.
GUIDING PRINCIPLES FOR CHRISTIAN CAMPING. National Sunday School Association, 1962.
Hammett, Catherine T.: A CAMP DIRECTOR TRAINS HIS OWN STAFF. Martinsville, Ind., American Camping Association, 1945.
Hammett, Catherine T., and Musselman, Virginia: THE CAMP PROGRAM BOOK. Association Press, 1951.
Hartwig, Marie, and Myers, Bettye: CHILDREN ARE HUMAN (EVEN AT CAMP), AND CHILDREN ARE HUMAN (IF THE COUNSELORS REALLY KNOW THEM). Minneapolis: Burgess Publishing Co., 1961, 1962.
Hartwig, Marie: WORKBOOK FOR CAMP COUNSELOR TRAINING. Minneapolis, Burgess Publishing Company, 1960.

Henderson, Luis M.: THE OUTDOOR GUIDE. Stackpole Co., 1950.
Hiltner, Seward: THE COUNSELOR IN COUNSELING. New York, Abingdon-Cokesbury Press, 1950.
Hood, Mary V.: OUTDOOR HAZARDS, REAL AND FANCIED. The Macmillan Co., 1955.
Hulme, William E.: GOD, SEX AND YOUTH. Englewood Cliffs, N.J., Prentice-Hall, 1959.
Hulme, William E.: HOW TO START COUNSELING. Englewood Cliffs, N.J., Prentice-Hall, 1959.
Hurlock, Elizabeth B.: ADOLESCENT DEVELOPMENT. McGraw-Hill Co., 1955.
Irwin, Frank L.: THE THEORY OF CAMPING—AN INTRODUCTION TO CAMPING IN EDUCATION. The Ronald Press Co., 1950.
Joy, Barbara Ellen: ANNOTATED BIBLIOGRAPHY ON CAMPING. Chicago, American Camping Association, 1950.
Joy, Barbara Ellen: CAMP CRAFT. Burgess Publishing Co., 1955.
Joy, Barbara Ellen: CAMPING. Burgess Publishing Co., 1957.
Joy, Barbara Ellen: COOPERATIVE COMMITTEE PLAN IN CAMPS. Camping Publications.
Joy, Barbara Ellen: PROFESSIONAL RELATIONSHIPS IN CAMP. Camp Publication, #6.
Joy, Barbara Ellen: SUGGESTIONS FOR RESPONSIBILITIES OF COUNSELORS FOR CARE OF CAMPERS. Camp Publication, #9.
Kesting, Ted: THE OUTDOOR ENCYCLOPEDIA. A. S. Barnes and Co., Inc., 1957.
Klein, Alan, and Irwin Haladner: IT'S WISE TO SUPERVISE. Toronto, Canadian Camping Association.
Knowles, Malcolm S., and Hilda F.: HOW TO DEVELOP BETTER LEADERS. New York, Association Press, 1955.
Koller, Larry: COMPLETE BOOK OF CAMPING AND THE OUTDOORS. Random House, Inc., 1957.
Kraus, Richard: RECREATION LEADER'S HANDBOOK. McGraw-Hill Book Co., 1955.
Laird, Donald A., and Laird, Eleanor C.: THE NEW PSYCHOLOGY FOR LEADERSHIP. McGraw-Hill Book Co.
Ledlie, John A., and Holbein, Francis W.: CAMP COUNSELOR'S MANUAL. Association Press, 1958.

Lindgren, Henry Clay: EFFECTIVE LEADERSHIP IN HUMAN RELATIONS.

Lindholm, Major Mauno A.: CAMPING AND OUTDOOR FUN. Hart Publishing Co., 1959.

Lynn, Gordon: CAMPING AND CAMP CRAFTS. Golden Books, 1959.

MacInnes, Gordon A.: A GUIDE TO WORSHIP IN CAMP AND CONFERENCE. The Westminster Press.

Mattson, Lloyd D.: CAMPING GUIDEPOSTS: CHRISTIAN CAMP COUNSELOR'S HANDBOOK. Chicago, Moody Press, 1962.

Menninger, William C.: HOW TO BE A SUCCESSFUL TEEN-AGER. Sterling Publishing Co., Inc., 1954.

Mitchell, A. Viola, and Crawford, Ida B.: CAMP COUNSELING. Philadelphia. W. B. Saunders Co., 1961.

Morris, C. Eugene: COUNSELING WITH YOUNG PEOPLE. Association Press, 1954.

Moser, Clarence G.: UNDERSTANDING BOYS AND UNDERSTANDING GIRLS. New York, Association Press, 1953, 1957.

Ott, Elmer: SO YOU WANT TO BE A CAMP COUNSELOR. New York, Association Press, 1946.

Peterson, Doris T.: YOUR FAMILY GOES CAMPING. Abingdon Press, 1959.

Radler, D. H., and Remmers, H. H.: THE AMERICAN TEEN-AGER. New York, Bobbs-Merrill Co., 1957.

Raymer, Mrs. Ralph H.: THE COUNSELORS JOB AT CAMP. Ontario Camping Assn.

Roberts, Dorothy M.: LEADERSHIP OF TEEN-AGE GROUPS. Association Press, 1950.

Robertson, Margaret M.: BECOMING A CAMP COUNSELOR. Chicago, Elizabeth McCormick Memorial Fund, 1949.

Rubin, Robert: THE BOOK OF CAMPING. Association Press, New York, 1949.

Soderholm, Marjorie Elaine: UNDERSTANDING THE PUPIL. Part II, The Primary and Junior Child and Part III, The Adolescent. Grand Rapids, Baker Book House, 1958.

Soifer, Margaret: FIRELIGHT ENTERTAINMENTS. Association Press, New York, 1944.

Soloman, B. L.: THE PROBLEM BOY. Oceana Publications.

Swanson, William E.: CAMPING FOR ALL IT'S WORTH. The Macmillan Co., 1952.

Todd, Floyd and Pauline: CAMPING FOR CHRISTIAN YOUTH. New York, Harper and Row, Publishers, 1963.
Trecker, Audrey R., and Harleight B.: HOW TO WORK WITH GROUPS. Association Press, 1952.
The United Presbyterian Church U.S.A.: THE YOUNG ADOLESCENT IN THE CHURCH. Board of Christian Education.
Webb, Kenneth B. (Editor): LIGHT FROM A THOUSAND CAMPFIRES. New York, Association Press, 1960.
Wentzel, Fred D., and Schlingman, Edward L.: THE COUNSELOR'S JOB. Association Press.
Wise, Carroll: PASTORAL COUNSELING: IT'S THEORY AND PRACTICE. Harper & Bros. Publishing, 1951.
Wittenberg, Rudolph: ADOLESCENCE AND DISCIPLINE. New York, Association Press, 1959.
Wittenberg, Rudolph: HOW TO HELP PEOPLE. Association Press, 1959.
Wittenberg, Rudolph: ON CALL FOR YOUTH. New York, Association Press, 1955.
ROLE PLAYING IN LEADERSHIP TRAINING AND GROUP PROBLEM SOLVING. New York, Association Press, 1956.

MAGAZINE ARTICLES

Doherty, J. Kenneth: COUNSELOR RATING SCALE. Camping Magazine, American Camping Association, February, 1950.
Flynn, Eansythe Rowley: CAMPING FOR 5 TO 8'S—IT PRESENTS ITS OWN CHALLENGE. Camping Magazine, American Camping Association, May, 1956.
Friedrich, John S.: SOCIOGRAMS PROVIDE GRAPHIC PICTURE OF CAMPER GROUP RELATIONS. Camping Magazine, American Camping Association, January, 1953.
Goodrich, Lois: AGE LEVEL CHARACTERISTICS OF CAMPERS. Recreation, March, 1957.
Healy, Edward M.: LEADERSHIP—SOME AIMS FOR THE FUTURE. Camping Magazine, American Camping Association, February, 1956.
Josselyn, Dr. Irene: PSYCHOLOGICAL NEEDS OF THE OVERPRIVILEGED CHILD. Camping Magazine, American Camping Association, June, 1952.
Lane, Howard A.: YOUR ROLE IN CAMPER DEVELOP-

MENT. Camping Magazine, American Camping Association, March, 1956.
Leonard, A. T., and van Hartesveldt, Fred: HOW UNDERSTANDING CHILD BEHAVIOR CAN IMPROVE COUNSELOR - CAMPER RELATIONSHIP. Camping Magazine, American Camping Association, January, 1957.
Link, Robert E.: WHAT MAKES A GOOD COUNSELOR. Camping Magazine, American Camping Association, January, 1951.
MacPeek, Walter: THE COUNSELOR I WANT FOR MY SON. Camping Magazine, American Camping Association, February, 1953.
Ransom, John E.: A GOOD BASIS FOR COUNSELOR EVALUATION. Camping Magazine, American Camping Association, January, 1952.
Rehwinkel, Jeanne: HEARING WHAT CAMPERS SAY. Camping Magazine, American Camping Association, January, 1952.
Rubin, Larry: THE CAMPER'S VIEW. Camping Magazine, American Camping Association, June, 1953.

FILMS

ARTIFICIAL RESPIRATION–6 min. Step-by-step demonstration of the new Back-Pressure Arm-Lift methods. (United States Dept. of Agriculture).

AXEMANSHIP–9 min., sd., b&w. Peter McLarin demonstrates the use and care of various types of axes. How to chop down a tree, split logs, and cut firewood. (Boy Scouts).

BOATS, MOTORS AND PEOPLE–30 min., sd., b&w or color. Emphasis on safety. (American Red Cross)

CAMP TIME, ANY TIME!–22 min., sd., color. Camping including nature mobile, rock collecting, clearing a stream, weather station, clay firing, canoeing, waterfront, trail signs, primitive unit, songs, etc. (Girl Scouts)

CAMPING EDUCATION–2 reels, sd., b&w, (college and adult). The program at National Camp for training professional camp leaders. (Life).

CANOE COUNTRY–15 min., sd., color (elementary-college). The Watsons take a canoe trip along an old fur route. Fishing, swimming, and setting up camp. Keeping matches dry, how to use campfires safely, and how to carry a canoe. (National Film Board of Canada).

COUNSELOR TRAINING FILMSTRIPS—(Y.M.C.A. Program Services). Based on the Y.M.C.A. Camp Counselor's Manual by Ledlie and Holbein, Association Press.

FIRST AID FUNDAMENTALS—10 min., sd., 1953, (junior high). Skin wounds, burns, sprains, bruises. Back-Pressure, Arm Lift method of artificial respiration. (Coronet).

HELP WANTED—22 min. Basic principles of first aid and caring for victims before the doctor arrives. Prepared under the supervision of prominent physicians and surgeons. (U.S. Public Health Service).

LIFE'S SUMMER CAMP—1948, 20 min., sound, b&w, (junior high—senior high—college). Shows training of teachers, administration and youth leaders. (Life, loan).

OVERNIGHT—2 reels, color or b&w, (junior high-college). Group and leader plan and enjoy overnight camping trip. All participate in group planning. (Girl Scouts).

THE ART OF BUILDING A FIRE—15 slides, showing proper sequence of steps in building a fire. (Wards)

WILDERNESS DAY—29 min., color. Canoe and camping trip on the lakes of Northern Minnesota with preparation of shelters, handling fires, cooking, waste disposal, proper canoe handling. (U. of Minn.).

YOUTH IN CAMPS—2 reels, sd., (college) Decentralized, "Camptivity" plan of camping. (Life).

INDEX